OP 91

IO

S0-BGD-715

FOUNDATIONS OF MODERN HISTORY

General Editor, A. Goodwin

Professor of Modern History, The University of Manchester

FOUNDATIONS OF MODERN HISTORY

The Government of Elizabethan England

by ALAN G. R. SMITH

Lecturer in History, The University of Glasgow

W · W · NORTON & COMPANY · INC ·
NEW YORK

General Preface

THIS series of short historical studies has as its main theme successive phases in the evolution of modern history from Renaissance times to the present day. Its general purpose is to provide within a limited compass, and at a reasonable cost, scholarly surveys of some of the fundamental developments which have influenced the civilization and conditioned the outlook of the modern world. A second aim of the series will be to illustrate how not only the general direction of recent historical inquiry but also its very content and its relations with other disciplines have been progressively modified. If students of scientific or technological subjects who are extending their interests to the 'liberal' arts or social sciences are made aware of these trends something will have been done to close the gap between the scientific and human cultures. A further feature of the series will be the endeavour to present selected periods of British history against the contemporary background of European development, with special emphasis on the nature and extent of cultural, scientific or intellectual interchange. Here the object will be to demonstrate the unity as well as the diversity of the European heritage and to re-examine its evolving significance in the context of global history.

During the last generation the researches of such notable scholars as Sir John Neale, Professors R. B. Wernham, S. T. Bindoff and J. Hurstfield have given a fresh impetus to the study of the aims, methods and effectiveness of English government in the second half of the sixteenth century. Much of this work has given historians a fresh understanding of the precise role played by Queen Elizabeth herself, her ministers, privy councillors, parliaments and court favourites in the formulation of policy and in the routine work of administration by official and unofficial civil servants and unpaid magistrates. Recent research has also thrown new light on the evolution and functioning of such institutions as the Exchequer, the court of Chancery and the courts of Wards and Requests and has drawn attention to the importance of the patronage system and of factions in the struggle for power both at the centre and in the localities. In the sphere of local government the relative significance of the declining office of sheriff, of the Tudor creation of lords lieutenant and their deputies and of the justices of the peace has been more accurately assessed and the vital administrative and 'police' functions performed by regional conciliar government in Wales and the Marches and the North have been studied in greater depth. These advances have, however, not removed the Elizabethan period from the field of controversy, for the debate on the so-called 'Tudor revolution' in government under Henry VIII and on the origins of the constitutional struggles between Crown and Parliament in the early seventeenth century still continues and the significance of the intervening period can thus be seen to be crucial.

This volume by Dr. A. G. R. Smith provides a balanced and judicious survey of the whole field of Elizabethan government and will, it is hoped, serve to introduce students and the interested general reader both to the more recent advances in scholarship and to the more general interpretations which they have suggested. It lays particular emphasis, in its exposition of institutional development, on the problems of internal and external security, the repercussions of the religious crisis and on the ever-present financial anxieties which perplexed Elizabethan governments; it clarifies the nature and limitations of the state's concern for the social and economic welfare of the population, and explains cogently the reasons for the comparative decline in the prestige and effectiveness of the Elizabethan system of government in its later stages. The conflict of powerful personalities, the effects of economic recessions and the struggle with Spain are here seen as determining factors in this important transitional stage in the evolution of English government.

Author's Note

Although a few paragraphs of this little book reflect my own researches, by far the greater part of it is a result of reading and reflecting on the work of others. The debt which I owe to the leading authorities on Tudor history will be as obvious as the fact that I do not always agree with their interpretations.

In quotations from manuscripts and printed sources I have modernized spelling, punctuation and capitalization.

I wish to thank my friend and colleague Mr. G. B. A. M. Finlayson for reading the book in typescript and making valuable comments; also Professor Goodwin, the general editor of the series, for his help and consideration. Finally I owe a special debt to Miss Pat Ferguson for typing the index.

University of Glasgow   April, 1967   A.G.R.S.

Contents

Chapter

Abbreviations

The following abbreviations are used in the footnotes:

APC	*Acts of the Privy Council*
Cheyney, i, ii.	E. P. Cheyney, *A History of England from the defeat of the Armada to the death of Elizabeth* (2 vols., 1914, 1926)
EcHR	*Economic History Review*
EHR	*English Historical Review*
Neale, *Commons*	J. E. Neale, *The Elizabethan House of Commons* (1949)
Neale, *Parliaments*, i	J. E. Neale, *Elizabeth I and her Parliaments 1559–1581* (1953)
Neale, *Parliaments*, ii	J. E. Neale, *Elizabeth I and her Parliaments 1584–1601* (1957)
Notestein	W. Notestein, *The Winning of the Initiative by the House of Commons* (British Academy Raleigh Lecture in History, reprinted from the Proceedings of the Academy, 1924)

CHAPTER ONE

The Queen

ON 21 November 1558 four days after Elizabeth's accession to the throne, Count de Feria, Spanish ambassador in England, reported to his master Philip II that the new Queen was 'very much wedded to the people and thinks as they do'. In another letter, written in the following month, he stated that she was 'incomparably more feared than her sister and gives her orders and has her way as absolutely as her father did'.[1] Feria's judgments of English affairs were by no means always sound, but his words on these two occasions enshrine truths. The first remark reflects the Queen's realization of the fact that one of the keys to successful rule lay in skilful propaganda, in winning and keeping the affections of the people as a whole. The second illustrates her determination to make her own decisions: there were to be no mayors in the Elizabethan palace. Feria's comments in fact direct attention to the twin pillars on which the Elizabethan system of government rested, the mystique of monarchy and its exploitation by the Queen on the one hand, and the practical part which Elizabeth played in affairs of state on the other.

In the sixteenth century few Englishmen questioned the right of the prince to command and their own duty to obey or at least not to resist such orders. This attitude of mind is exemplified in the famous *Mirror for Magistrates*, a collection of stories in verse and prose first published in 1559 and reprinted six times in the following eighteen years:

> Full little know we wretches what we do
> When we presume our princes to resist.
> We war with God against His glory too,
> That placeth in His office whom He list.
> Therefore was never traitor yet but missed
> The mark he shot at, and came to fearful end,
> Nor ever shall till God be forced to bend.

---

[1] *Calendar of State Papers Spanish*, 1558–67, pp. 4, 7.

And again:

> Who that resisteth his dread sovereign lord,
> Doth damn his soul by God's own very word.
> A Christian subject should with honour due
> Obey his sovereign though he were a Jew.[1]

The God-given powers of the Crown were in theory independent of worldly pomp and circumstance, but Elizabeth realized the political value of a magnificent court which reflected not merely her own glory but the majesty of England. Paul Hentzner, a German traveller who visited the court at Greenwich towards the end of the reign, left one of the best descriptions we possess of it. He was admitted by the Lord Chamberlain's permission to the presence chamber, through which the Queen was about to pass on her way to chapel. In due course Elizabeth emerged from her private apartments accompanied by a numerous suite.

First went gentlemen, barons, earls, knights of the garter, all richly dressed and bare-headed; next came the Chancellor, bearing the seals in a red silk purse, between two [attendants], one of which carried the royal sceptre, the other the sword of state in a red scabbard studded with golden *fleurs de lys*, the point upwards; next came the Queen ... very majestic. ... She had in her ears two pearls with very rich drops ..., upon her head she had a small crown, reported to be made of some of the gold of the celebrated Lunebourg table ...; and she had on a necklace of exceeding fine jewels. ... That day she was dressed in white silk, bordered with pearls of the size of beans, and over it a mantle of black silk shot with silver threads; her train was very long, the end of it borne by a marchioness. Instead of a chain she had an oblong collar of gold and jewels. As she went along in all this state and magnificence she spoke very graciously, first to one, then to another, whether foreign ministers or those who attended for different reasons. ... Whoever speaks to her it is kneeling [though] now and then she raises some with her hand. ...

The ladies of the Court followed next to her, very handsome and well-shaped, and for the most part dressed in white. She was guarded on each side by the gentlemen pensioners, fifty in number, with gilt battle-axes. In the ante chapel ... petitions were presented to her, and she received them most graciously, which occasioned the acclamation of, 'Long live Queen Elizabeth!' She answered it with, 'I thank you, my good people.' In the chapel was excellent music. As soon as it and the service was over ... the Queen returned in the same state and order and prepared to go to dinner.

---

[1] Cited by C. Morris, *Political Thought in England: Tyndale to Hooker* (Oxford, 1953), p. 70.

But while she was still at prayers, we saw her table set out with the following solemnity. A gentleman entered the room bearing a rod, and along with him another who had a tablecloth, which, after they had both kneeled three times with the utmost veneration, he spread upon the table, and, after kneeling again, they both retired. Then came two others, one with the rod again, the other with a salt-cellar, a plate, and bread. When they had kneeled, as the others had done, and placed what was brought upon the table, they too retired with the same ceremonies performed by the first. At last came an unmarried lady (we were told she was a countess), and along with her a married one, bearing a tasting knife. The former was dressed in white silk, who, when she had prostrated herself three times in the most graceful manner approached the table and rubbed the plates with bread and salt, with as much awe as if the Queen had been present. When they had waited there a little while the yeomen of the guard entered, bareheaded, clothed in scarlet, with a golden rose upon their backs, bringing in at each turn a course of twenty-four dishes served in plate, most of it gilt. These dishes were received by a gentleman in the same order they were brought and placed upon the table, while the lady taster gave to each of the guard a mouthful to eat of the particular dish he had brought, for fear of any poison. . . . At the end of all this ceremonial a number of unmarried ladies appeared, who, with particular solemnity, lifted the meat off the table and conveyed it into the Queen's inner and more private chamber.[1]

Such pageantry within the royal palaces must have been an imposing sight for the comparatively limited number of people who were able to witness it, but the Queen never forgot the need to charm and impress a wider circle among her subjects. She contrived to do this during her frequent progresses. In summer the Court often moved from the immediate vicinity of London, sometimes to outlying royal castles or manors, sometimes to enjoy the hospitality of provincial towns or of the nobility and gentry at their country seats. Such occasions were partly holidays, but they were also exercises in political propaganda, journeys on which the Queen exercised to the full her graciousness and did a great deal to cement those bonds of personal affection and loyalty between herself and her people upon which so much of the success of her domestic statecraft rested.

Henry Machyn, a Londoner who kept a diary of the early years of Elizabeth's reign, has left a description of the Queen's departure from the City in July 1561, when she set out on a progress through

[1] P. Hentzner, *A Journey into England in the Year 1598*, ed. Horace Walpole (Strawberry Hill, 1757), pp. 48-53.

Essex, Suffolk, and Hertfordshire. The scene must have been a splendid one, as the houses adjoining the processional route had been hung with cloths of gold and silver, with velvets and with precious silks. The Queen was attended by a magnificent train of heralds, knights and lords, as well as by the Lord Mayor and aldermen of London. The gentlemen pensioners in their colourful uniforms formed her bodyguard.[1] The sovereign's temporary farewell to her capital was not the only aspect of a progress which retained the pomp and solemnity of a state occasion. At the boundary of each shire she was received formally by the sheriff and principal gentlemen of the county, who often accompanied her throughout her whole stay in the locality, and each time she visited a town the corporation, in full regalia, assembled to pay its respects. The Queen, however, was the last person to forget that one of the principal reasons for her journeys was to maintain contact with the common people, who lined the roads along which the royal procession passed. The acclamation of her loyal subjects filled her with delight and the Spanish ambassador, writing in 1568, described how she sometimes 'ordered her carriage . . . to be taken where the crowd seemed thickest, and stood up and thanked the people'.[2]

The Queen displayed her graciousness to the full during a visit to Warwick in August 1572. She approached the town at 3 o'clock on the afternoon of the 12th accompanied in her coach by Lady Warwick and attended by numerous other lords and ladies. The dignitaries of the town, the Bailiff, the Recorder and the principal burgesses, awaited her on their knees. When the royal procession stopped beside this reception committee she ordered 'every part and side of the coach to be opened' so that all the onlookers might see her clearly, 'which most gladly they desired'. Then, 'after a pause made, the . . . Recorder began his oration to her Majesty'. This discourse, which contained fulsome praise of the Queen's happy government as well as an account of the history of Warwick, must have taken some time to deliver – in its printed version it occupies five large pages – but Elizabeth gave no hint of the boredom which she may have felt. Indeed, later in the proceedings she called to the Recorder, 'come hither, little

[1] *The Diary of Henry Machyn*, ed. J. G. Nichols (*Camden Society Publication*, xlii, 1848), pp. 263–4.
[2] Cited J. E. Neale, *Queen Elizabeth* (Bedford Ed., 1938), p. 207.

Recorder', and giving him her hand to kiss said, 'It was told me that you would be afraid to look upon me, or to speak boldly, but you were not so [a]fraid of me as I was of you'.[1] It was such small but unforgettable gestures, made in the sight and in the hearing of many of her subjects, which created and maintained the image of a Queen who was always a figure of majesty but who nevertheless contrived to retain the common touch.

Progresses did not take place every year and they were almost completely suspended for the whole troublesome decade before the Armada. In the 1590's, however, the custom was revived. The ageing Elizabeth refused to admit that she was getting too old to travel and even in the very last summer of her life – the summer of 1602 – she made a short journey which took her to Middlesex and Buckinghamshire. It is worth noting that the Queen never visited the west country, the north or Wales. The progresses were confined to the south and the midlands where the main strength of her régime lay.[2] It would be fanciful to argue that frequent journeys by the Queen to the north would have made her government as popular there as it was in the more prosperous southern half of her realm, but it would be wrong too to minimize the effect which the sovereign's presence could produce when she appeared at her most regal and yet at the same time most human in the midst of her subjects. It is fair to conclude that Elizabeth's frequent journeys were an important help in creating and maintaining her popularity in those parts of the realm which she visited.

The Queen's progresses, the elaborate pomp of the Court within the royal palaces, the mystique of monarchy: these taken together go some way to explaining the hold which Elizabeth's government exercised over the minds of her subjects. The charm of the sovereign and splendid pageantry were however aids to good government, not substitutes for it. In the last resort the Queen's success depended on the wisdom of her policies, on her fundamental abilities as a ruler. She certainly succeeded to the throne with one great and obvious handicap: she was a woman. Only a few months before her accession John Knox had published his *First Blast of the Trumpet against the Monstrous Regiment of Women.*

---

[1] J. Nichols ed., *The Progresses of Queen Elizabeth*, i (1823), pp. 309–16.
[2] E. K. Chambers, *The Elizabethan Stage*, i (Oxford, 1923), pp. 119–20.

In this he wrote that, 'to promote a woman to bear rule, super-
iority, dominion or empire above any realm, nation or city is
repugnant to nature; contumely to God, a thing most contrary
to his revealed will and approved ordinance; and finally, it is the
subversion of good order, of all equity and justice'. He backed up
his argument from the Bible, the Fathers and the Classics and
stated that men were less than beasts to permit such an inversion
of God's order, 'for no man ever saw the lion make obedience and
stoop before the lioness, neither yet can it be proved that the hind
takes the conducting of the herd amongst the harts'.[1] Now it is
true that Knox's *Blast* was specifically directed against two
Catholic women rulers, Mary Tudor of England and the Queen
Regent of Scotland, Mary of Guise, but the sentiments which he
expressed were acceptable to most men of his day. The second half
of the sixteenth century was prolific in women rulers, Mary
Tudor and Elizabeth in England; Mary of Guise and Mary
Queen of Scots in Scotland; Margaret of Parma in the Netherlands; Catherine de Medici in France. With the exception of
Elizabeth, they must all be accounted failures. This may be
hardly surprising in view of the general prejudice against women
in power, but it does make Elizabeth's success all the more
striking. To grasp the reasons for that success it is necessary to
understand, on the one hand, the broad policies which the Queen
pursued and, on the other, the personal part which she played in
day to day administration.

There is no doubt that Elizabeth took a direct interest in all
aspects of administration. Her interference in minor matters
sometimes irritated her ministers beyond measure. She even
criticized the wording of the commission to try Mary Queen of
Scots. 'I would to God,' wrote Sir Francis Walsingham to Lord
Burghley on that occasion that 'her Majesty could be content to
refer these things to them that can best judge of them as other
princes do.'[2] Such interventions by the Queen might be annoying
and uncomfortable for ministers and officials, but they did keep
the Crown's servants on their toes. Sir John Neale has made a
happy comparison between the Queen's part in government and

[1] *The Works of John Knox*, ed. David Laing, iv (Edinburgh, 1855), pp. 373,
393.
[2] C. Read, *Mr. Secretary Walsingham and Queen Elizabeth*, iii (Oxford, 1925),
p. 52 note 4.

the part played by Sir Winston Churchill during the Second World War.[1] Churchill was famous for the minutes and memoranda, containing requests for information or reproofs, which he dispatched in all directions. Elizabeth's methods were somewhat similar, though her inquiries and reprimands were likely to be verbal, whereas a very large proportion of his were written.

Though the Queen was likely to interfere personally at any time in any aspect of administration she did not allow herself to become too involved in trivial details. She did not try to do everything herself. Indeed, an important part of her genius lay in her ability to pick good advisers (men like Burghley, Walsingham and Robert Cecil) to whom she generally allowed a wide initiative in routine affairs. She did, however, tend to take the credit for herself when affairs went well and to blame her ministers when they went badly. On occasion even Burghley's monumental patience was tried beyond measure by her unfairness, as in November 1588 when he wrote to Walsingham, 'All irresolutions . . . are thrown upon us two in all her speeches to everybody. The wrong is intolerable.'[2] Clearly it was necessary to have a thick skin to be one of Elizabeth's advisers!

The direct personal interest which the Queen took in all aspects of administration and her ability to pick good ministers and delegate authority to them in routine matters were admirable qualities, but everything in the last resort depended on whether her policies were wise. The Queen depended in some measure upon her councillors for advice in the formulation of broad government policy, though the fundamentally important question of the extent of that dependence is bedevilled by the difficulty of interpreting such evidence as exists. Yet however much she may have relied upon ministers for advice and ideas, she alone made the final decisions. In the last analysis credit for the triumphs of the period must therefore go to Elizabeth herself. Her reign was, in the broadest sense, successful because she avoided important defeats in foreign wars, civil war at home and state bankruptcy by a judicious mixture of economy, moderation, prevarication and conservatism.

Economy was absolutely essential if the Queen was to avoid

[1] J. E Neale, *Essays in Elizabethan History* (1958), p. 37.
[2] Cited by Cheyney, i, p. 12.

bankruptcy because, throughout the reign, her revenue was extremely limited. Fortunately Elizabeth had admirable sense in money matters. Her principles were those of sound business, to pay what she owed and spend what she could afford. Nothing infuriated her more than bad financial management. This is admirably illustrated by her attitude to the English expedition sent to the Netherlands in 1585 to fight against Spain. Its commander, the Earl of Leicester, had no trace of financial ability: he knew only how to spend, and Elizabeth bewailed the slackness and corruption which attended the payment of her troops. The expedition, she complained to Leicester in 1586, had become 'a sieve, that spends as it receives to little purpose'.[1]

There can be no doubt indeed that it was largely due to the personal and unremitting vigilance of the Queen that England escaped financial disaster. Between 1558 and 1570 her ordinary revenue – consisting principally of rents from royal lands, feudal incidents, customs dues, the first fruits of benefices, and the profits of justice – averaged only about £200,000 per annum. Parliamentary subsidies brought in another £50,000 a year and the sale of Crown lands a further £15,000, making a total annual revenue of approximately £265,000. By the last years of the reign revenue had increased considerably. During the period 1590 to 1603 it reached an average of about £490,000 per annum, of which £300,000 came from ordinary revenue, £135,000 from parliamentary taxation, £40,000 from land sales and £15,000 from prizes taken at sea. During the last years of the reign, however, Elizabeth, besides conducting naval operations against Spain, was fighting very expensive wars in France and Ireland. Indeed, in view of the enormous demands upon her purse during these later years and the still comparatively limited resources she had to deal with them, it is astonishing that she managed to stay solvent. She was able to do so, in fact, only because she cut ordinary expenditure to the bone and was thus able to save about £100,000 a year from her ordinary revenue. This, together with parliamentary subsidies and the money from land sales and prizes she used to finance the English war effort. She died not more and perhaps substantially less than £350,000 in debt – a remarkable

[1] *Calendar of State Papers Foreign*, 1586–87, p. 195. On the expedition generally see J. E. Neale, 'Elizabeth and the Netherlands, 1586–7,' *EHR*, xlv (1930), pp. 373–96.

achievement in the circumstances.[1] Elizabeth's economy was certainly one of the principal reasons for the success of her government.

Equally important was the Queen's moderation. She was so obviously reluctant to adopt inquisitorial methods, so clearly anxious to avoid bloodshed if at all possible, that, despite the frequent treason trials of her reign, she has never gained the sanguinary reputation of her sister and her father. Perhaps the most striking examples of her moderation can be seen in her religious policy. One episode, which reveals her attitude to her Catholic subjects, may serve to illustrate this point. When the Parliament of 1571 met it was, not unnaturally, fanatically anti-Catholic. The Northern Rebellion of 1569 and the Papal Bull of 1570 excommunicating and deposing Elizabeth had fanned the flames of Protestant intolerance. In this atmosphere a bill which compelled reception of Anglican communion at least once a year under penalty of a fine of 100 marks (nearly £67) was introduced in the Commons, in order, as one Puritan zealot declared, that 'not only the external and outward show', but 'the very secrets of the heart' should be revealed. This, of course, was because no genuine Catholic could possibly take communion in an Anglican Church. The bill passed both houses with the cordial support of most of the bishops and probably that of the Privy Council as well, but the Queen vetoed it.[2] She had always said that she would not make 'windows into men's souls'. She did think it right that all should be compelled to attend ordinary church services; that was a matter of outward conformity. It was a different thing to require attendance at communion; that would be forcing men's consciences. Here we can see that Elizabeth held true to her principle of moderation even at the time of the most violent anti-Catholic feeling and in face of very different views held by her chief advisers in Church and state. Her objective was to preserve English unity by refusing to allow passions to get out of hand. She saw, probably rightly, the risk of civil conflict if she gave her approval to extreme measures. Moderation in most things: that

[1] It is very difficult to determine fairly the exact extent of the Queen's indebtedness at the time of her death. See W. R. Scott, *The Constitution and Finance of English, Scottish and Irish Joint Stock Companies*, iii (Cambridge, 1911), pp. 494, 495, 498, 507, 508; F. C. Dietz, *English Public Finance 1558–1641* (New York, 1932), p. 113.

[2] Neale, *Parliaments*, i, pp. 192, 215–16.

philosophy was one of the bases of the Queen's policy, one of the keys to the success of her government. Significantly it is also one of the main themes of a recent important interpretation of the Queen's life and reign.[1]

Elizabeth, who hated extreme measures, was often reluctant to commit herself irrevocably to *any* course of action in an important matter. There is no doubt, in fact, that prevarication was one of her outstanding characteristics. This can be seen very clearly in her attitude to the succession to the throne. In her second Parliament, that of 1563, strong pressure was brought to bear upon her to name a successor in case she should die without heirs, and agitation on the subject continued for much of the rest of her life. Her answers to parliamentary petitions on the subject were masterpieces of evasion. 'As soon as there may be a convenient time . . . I will deal therein for your safety,' she told a delegation of Lords and Commons in 1566.[2] That was indeed an 'answer answerless', for, as we know now, the Queen never thought the time 'convenient'. Her attitude has been interpreted as masterly indecision and also as sheer stupidity. The Elizabethan House of Commons certainly thought it was the latter and constantly bewailed the horrors that would befall the country if the Queen died without heirs and without establishing the succession. Civil war, they thought, would be the result: 'the waste of noble houses, the slaughter of people, subversion of towns, intermission of all things pertaining to the maintenance of the realm, unsurety of all men's possessions, lives, and estates, daily interchange of attainders and treasons.'[3] Elizabeth, however, saw equally clearly the dangers of naming an heir during her lifetime. This could produce strife while she was alive (the nominated successor and the disappointed contenders might all become the focus of plots against her government) without necessarily avoiding civil war after her death. Her attitude was certainly not stupid, but neither was her policy masterly indecision. She realized that she was taking a calculated risk, gambling on living long enough for time to solve the problem. Of course, time did. By 1603 James VI of Scotland was the obvious heir. Elizabeth's inherent tendency to

---

[1] By J. Hurstfield, *Elizabeth I and the Unity of England* (1960).

[2] Neale, *Parliaments*, i, p. 150.

[3] *Ibid.*, 106

prevarication had its dangers, but it is arguable that, in the matter of the succession at least, it represented the lesser of two evils.

A fourth characteristic of her government – one which appears very clearly in her attitude to war and to the administrative machinery – was conservatism. The Queen fundamentally detested the whole idea of war. A decisive war, she realized, would destroy the world which she knew and produce a new and possibly more unwelcome international situation. This attitude reflected the Queen's deep political conservatism, which made her prefer to try and live with problems rather than attempt fundamental solutions.

Her reluctance to commit herself to war can be seen in her attitude in 1585 when she sent an army to the Low Countries. She looked on this as a defensive measure to prevent the seemingly impending subjugation of the Netherlands by Spain, a subjugation which would be an intolerable threat to English security. She had no desire for the extension of English territorial power on the continent and hoped by her intervention merely to force Philip II to grant his subjects in the Low Countries the kind of position they had enjoyed under his father, the Emperor Charles V – nominal subjection to Habsburg sovereignty but a wide degree of practical freedom. With this aim in mind she flatly refused the Dutch envoy's offer of sovereignty over the rebel states, and when the Earl of Leicester, her lieutenant in the Netherlands, thanked the Dutch for a similar offer she issued an immediate order that he should 'not accept the same'.[1] Even in 1585, in fact, she was hoping to avoid open war with Spain. The hope was illusory, but it does show how her mind worked.

Elizabeth's attitude towards administration, too, was extremely conservative. There is no evidence that she ever considered any substantial changes or innovations in the machinery of government in the Church or in the central administration of the state. In the Church, as a result of her settlement, the familiar judicial and financial institutions were preserved in their traditional, often unsatisfactory forms, though with diminished prestige. The Queen, however, was philosophical about the situation. 'Thus much I must say,' she told Parliament in 1585, 'that some faults and negligences may grow and be [in the Church], as in all other

[1] *Calendar of State Papers Foreign*, 1585–86, p. 323.

great charges . . ., and what vocation without.'[1] Her attitude towards the central machinery of state seems to have been the same. There is no indication that she ever thought of making any substantial changes in an effort to achieve greater administrative efficiency.

To sum up, it can be said that by her economy the Queen avoided bankruptcy; by her moderation, especially in religious matters, she avoided the possibility of civil war; by her conservative attitude to the European situation she avoided reckless foreign adventures. These facts explain why, in the broadest sense, her government was a success. Yet there is a reverse side of the coin. By the 1590s at least one of her characteristics, her conservatism, was a positive drawback to the solution of pressing problems. In the last decade of the reign the government was faced with a severe economic depression as well as with difficulties over the war with Spain, over finance, and over the Crown's relations with Parliament. In this situation new ideas were essential, but the Queen had nothing new to offer, no feasible solution for the depression and the social distress which accompanied it; no ideas for bringing the war with Spain to an end; no solution to the financial problem except to make ever larger demands on Parliaments which showed themselves increasingly ready to challenge the royal prerogative.

In these last years of the reign there seems, in fact, to have been a general feeling of *fin de siècle*, a feeling heightened by the rebellion and execution in February 1601 of the people's hero, the brilliant and mercurial Earl of Essex. In these circumstances the Queen's death on 24 March 1603 came almost as a relief and the warmth of James I's reception in England – his journey from Edinburgh to London was a triumphal progress – reflected the fact that the people were glad to have a king again. Their joy soon evaporated when they got to know James better, but its reality in 1603 was a commentary on the last years of Elizabeth's government.

[1] S. D'Ewes, *The Journals of all the Parliaments during the reign of Queen Elizabeth* (1682), p. 328.

CHAPTER TWO

The Privy Council

THE Privy Council was hardly less important than the Queen in the government of Elizabethan England. It advised her on matters of policy and was also the central institution in the administration of the country. Despite these vitally important roles, however, its history in this period is largely unknown. We have at present 'only the generalizations inherited from the past or derived from a quick survey of such master records as are in print'.[1] This unhappy state of affairs is being remedied by research now in progress, but, until the results of that work appear, we must rely on existing knowledge and the printed register of the Council, unsatisfactory though these may be.

It can be said with some certainty, however, that one of the most significant facts about the Council was its size. It was a comparatively small body, much smaller than it had been under the Queen's predecessors, or was to be under her successors. In Edward VI's reign there were, at one time, as many as forty privy councillors, and under Mary the largest number was forty-four.[2] Councils of such size were unwieldy and therefore inefficient. Elizabeth realized this. On 20 November 1558, three days after her accession, addressing members of her sister's Privy Council and other prominent statesmen assembled at Hatfield she said:

For counsel and advice I shall accept you of my nobility and such others of you the rest as in consultation I shall think meet and shortly appoint; to the which also I will join to their aid and for ease of their burden others meet for my service. And they which I shall not appoint, let them not think the same for any disability in them, but for that I

---

[1] G. R. Elton, 'The Problems and Significance of Administrative History in the Tudor Period', *Journal of British Studies*, volume iv. No. 2 (May 1965), p. 23.

[2] J. R. Tanner, *Tudor Constitutional Documents* (2nd ed., Cambridge, 1930), pp. 217–18.

consider a multitude doth make rather discord and confusion than good counsel.[1]

These were wise words and the Queen acted on them. Through-out her reign there were never more than twenty privy councillors and for a short time in the 1590s there were as few as nine.[2] Her Council was at its largest during her early years but for most of the last decade of the century it numbered only thirteen.[3] Under the early Stuarts numbers started to grow again. By 1623 there were thirty-five privy councillors and in Charles I's reign a maximum of forty-two.[4] The early Stuart Council, just like the Council between 1547 and 1558, was too large to be efficient. In contrast, the much smaller Elizabethan body seems to have done its work very effectively.

Inevitably there was always a difference between the nominal size of the Council and the number of councillors present at any one meeting. During the years 1558 to 1570 the attendance was usually between five and eleven. In the 1590s it was generally between four and nine. Business in fact tended to be concentrated in the hands of a group of men who attended much more regularly than the others. In the early years of the reign – between 1558 and 1570 – the bulk of Council work seems to have fallen on Sir William Cecil, principal secretary and easily the most frequent attender; the Lord High Admiral, Edward, Lord Clinton, later Earl of Lincoln; Sir Francis Knollys, the Queen's cousin and Vicechamberlain of the Royal Household; Sir Edward Rogers, Comptroller of the Household; William, Lord Howard of Effingham, another relative of the Queen's, who held the office of Lord Chamberlain; Sir Nicholas Bacon, Lord Keeper of the Great Seal; Lord Robert Dudley, created Earl of Leicester in 1564, the Queen's favourite and Master of the Horse; and Sir Ambrose Cave, Chancellor of the Duchy of Lancaster. Between 1570 and 1590, Cecil, created Lord Burghley in 1571 and appoint-

[1] J. A Froude, *History of England*, vi (1875), pp. 120–21.

[2] Authorities differ as to the size of the Elizabethan Privy Council. Cheyney, i, 65, says that it was between 18 and 20; D. M. Gladish, *The Tudor Privy Council* (Retford, 1915), 29, says 17 or 18; G. R. Elton, *The Tudor Constitution*, (Cambridge, 1960), 92, says 12 to 18. The figures 9 to 20 are based upon an examination of the Council registers between 1558 and 1603.

[3] *APC* 1590–1604, *passim*.

[4] E. R. Turner, *The Privy Council of England in the Seventeenth and Eighteenth Centuries*, i (Baltimore, 1927), pp. 73, 79.

ed Lord Treasurer the following year, and Knollys, appointed
Treasurer of the Household in 1570, remained among those most
frequently present at meetings, as did Lincoln and Leicester until
their deaths in 1585 and 1588 respectively. In addition to these
stalwarts of the early Elizabethan Council three other men were
prominent attenders during the middle years of the reign: Sir
James Croft, Comptroller of the Household; Sir Francis Walsingham, appointed principal secretary and admitted to the Privy
Council in 1573; and Sir Christopher Hatton, made Vicechamberlain and privy councillor in 1577 and Lord Chancellor in
1587. During the last thirteen years of the reign those most diligent
in attendance seem to have been Sir Robert Cecil, who was sworn
of the Council in 1591 and became principal secretary in 1596;
Lord Buckhurst, appointed Lord Treasurer in 1599; Charles,
Lord Howard of Effingham, Lord High Admiral, created Earl
of Nottingham in 1597; Sir John Fortescue, Chancellor of the
Exchequer; Sir Thomas Egerton, privy councillor and Lord
Keeper of the Great Seal from 1596; and Sir William Knollys,
councillor and Comptroller of the Household, also from 1596. To
these names must be added that of Burghley, who was regularly
present at meetings until a month before his death in August
1598.[1] He had served on the Elizabethan Council as secretary
of state and then as Lord Treasurer for almost forty years – an
unparalleled record. On appointing him at the beginning of the
reign the Queen had said: 'I give you this charge that you shall
be of my Privy Council and content yourself to take pains for me
and my realm. . . .'[2] Burghley had indeed taken pains! His
diligence in the routine work of a privy councillor is a striking
illustration of his devoted service to Queen and country.

Burghley, however, was only the most notable of the distinguished ministers and officials who formed by far the most important element in the Elizabethan Council. At the beginning of the
reign, it is true, the Council included a number of 'magnates',
men who owed their influence at least as much to their broad
estates as to the Queen's favour. In 1563 there may have been as
many as six[3] of these out of a total of twenty. By the end of the

[1] *APC* 1558–1604, *passim.*
[2] J. A. Froude, *History of England*, vi, p. 121.
[3] The Duke of Norfolk, the Earls of Arundel, Bedford, Derby and Pembroke,
and Lord Clinton. All these men were substantial landowners. See L. Stone,
The Crisis of the Aristocracy 1558–1641 (Oxford, 1965), Appendix viii.

reign only one man, Gilbert, Earl of Shrewsbury, fell into this category out of a total of fourteen. The other thirteen were Archbishop Whitgift, the only ecclesiastic to play a prominent part as a councillor during Elizabeth's reign, and twelve great officers of state and of the Household, men who were on the Council because of their proven ability as advisers and administrators. In short, the Elizabethan Privy Council became an increasingly professional body as the reign progressed.[1]

It was also an itinerant body. It met wherever the Queen happened to be, following her on her journeys from Whitehall to other royal palaces and on her progresses throughout the country. This reflected the fact that one of its primary duties was to advise the sovereign. This was a duty, not a right. Elizabeth was quite prepared to transact important business without consulting her Council. In April 1586 Sir Francis Walsingham wrote to the Earl of Leicester, commander of the English forces in the Low Countries:

I have let my lords [of the Council] here understand how unkindly your lordship taketh it that you hear so seldom from them, and that since your charge there you never received any letter of advice from them. They answer, as it is truth, that, her Majesty retaining the whole direction of the causes of that country to herself and such advice as she recciveth underhand, they know not what to write or to advise. She can by no means, as I have heretofore written unto your lordship, endure that the causes of that country should be subject to any debate in Council, otherwise than as she herself shall direct, and therefore men forbear to do that which otherwise they would.[2]

Even when the Queen did ask the Council's advice she did not always take it. In the summer of 1562 she was proposing to travel to York to meet Mary Queen of Scots. Unfortunately the first French religious war had just broken out and such a meeting between Elizabeth and the Catholic claimant to the English succession might have been regarded as a blow to the Protestant cause. In June the Queen made one of her rare personal appearances at the Council Board to hear the whole question discussed. The speech made on that occasion by the Lord Keeper, Sir Nicholas Bacon, has come down to us. It was a firm rejection of the idea of a meeting. Bacon assumed that Mary, whatever

---

[1] *APC* 1558–70; 1601–1604, *passim.*
[2] *Correspondence of Robert Dudley, Earl of Leycester,* ed. J. Bruce, (*Camden Society Publication,* xxvii, 1844), p. 237.

she might say to the contrary, was under the control of her relatives of the House of Guise, who were then one of the dominant influences in France. The Guise were fanatically Catholic, and as discussions between sovereigns were so rare as to be regarded as 'manifestations of great amity' such a meeting, in the circumstances of the time, could not fail to help the Catholic party in France. He concluded: 'it is very evident that no hope of good and great fear of ill is to be conceived by this interview, and therefore for my part I cannot allow of it.' All the other councillors supported these arguments, but the Queen was not convinced. She replied to them 'with such fineness of wit and excellence of utterance as for the same she was commended; and not allowing replication, she concluded that if she had not such advertisement from Throckmorton [English ambassador in France], that justly might cause her to stay, go she would'. Her decision was 'groaned at and lamented of the most and wisest'.[1] Later the situation in France took a turn for the worse and Elizabeth put off the interview, but her behaviour in Council shows beyond all doubt that she was prepared to make her own decisions, even against the unanimous opinion of her leading advisers.

It would, of course, be absurd to imagine that the Privy Council, a body which consisted of the most influential men in the realm, each with strong views about the conduct of affairs, always presented a united front. The unanimity of the councillors in June 1562 was a rare occurrence. Throughout the reign, in fact, the Council was rent by faction. This was certainly so in the summer of 1567, when it seemed as though the Queen was on the point of marrying the Archduke Charles of Austria. The decision turned on whether or not Elizabeth was prepared to concede to him private exercise of the Catholic religion. Leicester's fate was bound up with the outcome. If the Queen married he would no longer hold his special position in the state. He thus worked desperately to avert the match, not hesitating to stir up Protestant passions in the process. Other councillors, Norfolk, Sussex and Cecil being the most prominent among them, were wholeheartedly in favour of the marriage. With her Council divided the Queen hesitated and in the end refused to concede Charles's demand. Cecil and his supporters were in despair. They accused

[1] J. A. Froude, *History of England*, vi, 567–71; *Calendar of State Papers Foreign*, 1562, p. 93.

Leicester and his followers of exploiting religious prejudices for selfish ends. 'If Protestants be but only Protestants!', wrote Sussex; 'but if some have a second intent which they cloak with religion, and place be given to their counsel, God defend the Queen with His mighty hand.'[1]

Leicester and his party were not so speedily successful, however, in the greatest of all issues which divided the Council in the high Elizabethan period, the question of whether or not to give military aid to the Dutch rebels in their struggle against Spain. Leicester's most formidable ally in this dispute was Sir Francis Walsingham, and his leading opponent was Cecil, who by that time had been created Lord Burghley. The Leicester–Burghley rivalry was in part a personal contest for political power between Queen Elizabeth's great favourite and her great minister, but there were also perfectly genuine divisions of policy between the two men. Burghley wanted peace, whereas Leicester favoured an active policy of intervention in the Netherlands, a lead eagerly followed by Walsingham, who wrote:

> What juster cause can a prince that maketh profession of the Gospel have to enter into wars than when he seeth confederacies made for the rooting out of the Gospel and religion he professeth? All creatures are created to advance God's glory; therefore, when this glory is called in question, no league nor policy can excuse if by all means he seek not the defense of the same, yea, with his life.

These differences of opinion communicated themselves to the Privy Council at large and from about 1578 two distinct groups are discernible among the councillors. One group, consisting of the Earls of Sussex and Lincoln, Sir Nicholas Bacon, Sir James Croft, and the Queen's cousin, Lord Hunsdon, supported Burghley. The other composed of Sir Francis Knollys, the Earls of Warwick and Bedford, Dr. Thomas Wilson, Sir Christopher Hatton, and Sir Thomas Bromley, followed the lead of Leicester and Walsingham.

It is clear that during the years 1578 to 1585 Leicester and his supporters on the Council outnumbered Burghley and his partisans. If the Queen's policy had been determined by counting the heads of her advisers England would certainly have intervened actively in the Low Countries during these years. Elizabeth, however, as has already been noted, followed the advice of the

[1] J. E. Neale, *Queen Elizabeth*, pp. 153–4

Council only when it suited her. She was essentially a woman of peace. Thus it was only in August 1585, when it looked as if the whole of the Netherlands was about to fall into Spanish hands, that she agreed to send troops to assist the Dutch rebels. The war party in the Council had triumphed at last, but only after a struggle lasting seven years during which it had constantly been thwarted by a smaller group of councillors who were able to command the Queen's support and thus keep England out of continental adventures.[1]

During the 1590s another faction struggle was played out in both the Privy Council and the country at large. In that conflict the role of Leicester was filled – though without any of Leicester's essential moderation – by the Earl of Essex, while Burghley's part was played by his younger son, Sir Robert Cecil. That struggle, however, is best examined in another context.[2]

So far we have considered the Council as an advisory body, but it was also the chief administrative and executive agency of the realm. In Mary's reign it had acquired a seal of its own and in the Elizabethan period there seem to have been two seals in use concurrently, each kept by one of the clerks of the Council. It is unlikely, however, that seals were applied to all Elizabethan council documents. They seem to have been used mainly to ensure the secrecy of individual letters or packets: 'the common practice was to fasten the flaps of the folded documents with wax. ... The seal was then impressed upon the outside in such a way that the document could not be opened and its contents discovered, without destroying the seal or tearing the paper.'[3]

To distribute its orders and letters the Council had the services of the messengers of the Chamber. By the end of the reign these numbered forty or more. Their duties must often have been unpleasant ones. In January 1592, for example, Thomas Michael, one of the messengers, was ordered to 'apprehend and bring before the Lords [of the Council] Sir William Woodhouse, knight'. Given the nature of their jobs dishonest messengers must have had plenty of opportunities to line their own pockets. One who did,

[1] C. Read, 'Walsingham and Burghley in Queen Elizabeth's Privy Council', *EHR*, xxviii (1913), pp. 34–58.

[2] See Chapter Five.

[3] L. W. Labaree and R. E. Moody, 'The Seal of the Privy Council', *EHR*, xliii (1928), pp. 195–9.

for a time at least, was John Norbury. In November 1591 the
Council wrote to Francis Hastings about 'certain lewd persons',
whom he had had arrested:

amongst the which there is one named Norbury, being an extraordinary
messenger [of the Chamber], and another called Nixon, who, giving
themselves forth by other names, have with counterfeit warrants, in most
lewd and slanderous manner exacted divers sums of money of sundry
persons, almost in all the counties of the realm. We have, therefore, for
their more exemplary and due punishment . . . thought good to require
you to cause the said Norbury and Nixon to be safely sent up hither under
safe custody.

The two culprits were censured in Star Chamber for their offences
but a year later they were up to their old tricks again. This time
they were imprisoned.[1]

It was of great importance that the Privy Council should be
able to trust its servants, for the messages they carried were
legion. The Council concerned itself with everything that went
on in England; its administrative and executive work was all
pervasive. On one typical day, 5 July 1574, it dealt with a private
quarrel between Sir Thomas Palmer and Thomas Stoughton;
arranged the journey which Count Swevingham, a Spanish agent,
planned to make to the west country; ordered reprisals against
Portugal for losses suffered by John Sambitores, a denizen of the
realm; discussed a case involving the non-payment of marine
insurance; sent orders to the commissioners for musters in
Worcestershire; made provisions for the trial of two cases of
murder; ordered the preparation of 200 troops for service in
Ireland; considered two complaints made by the French ambassador about the treatment of French subjects; ordered the release
of Thomas Watson, the deprived Bishop of Lincoln, then a prisoner in the Marshalsea; sent instructions to the Master of the
Rolls for the freeing of Prestall, a prisoner in the Queen's Bench
jail; wrote to the Warden of the Middle Marches about the
treatment of a Scottish refugee; ordered the Commissioners for
victuals in Wiltshire, Dorset, Sussex and Hampshire to provide
immediate help in supplying the Queen's navy; directed the vice-
admirals and other officers of the coastal shires to prevent the
departure of all private vessels until the Queen's ships had been

[1] *APC* 1591–92, pp. 65, 194; *APC* 1592, pp. 330, 344, 373.

properly manned and provisioned; granted the Treasurer of Berwick twenty days' leave of absence; sent a letter to the Regent of Scotland concerning good relations between the two countries; and dispatched warrants to the Treasurer and Chamberlains of the Exchequer for the payment of the Master of the Works and the Master Carpenter at Portsmouth. On 13 November 1597 the Council ordered the release of Sir John Savile, a prisoner in the Fleet; instructed the Treasurer of the Chamber to pay Sir Charles Percy £20 for military services; discussed the refusal of certain people in Worcestershire, Middlesex, Herefordshire and Berkshire to contribute to the forced loan of 1597; sent instructions to Sir John Higham about the treatment of recusants imprisoned under his care; made provision for the sale of the goods of Lord Burgh, late Lord Deputy of Ireland, who had died heavily in debt to the Queen; arranged for the payment of troops formerly in the Low Countries but recently returned to England; sent instructions to Sir John Wogan about the treatment of the crew of a captured Spanish ship; wrote to Sir Thomas Norris, President of Munster, about abuses of legal procedure in his province; ordered that Sir Thomas Tresham, a recusant imprisoned at Ely, should be temporarily released so that he could attend to his legal business; and considered a charge of lewd words made against William Holland of Sussex.[1]

These varied administrative acts can be classified under two headings, public and private. It was, of course, public matters, 'causes that concern her Majesty and the state of the realm', that the Council regarded as most important. Its concern in the broadest sense, for orderly government and for the security of the state was reflected in the multitude of orders which it sent throughout the reign to officials of all grades in all parts of the country and in the major role which it played after 1585 in the organization of offensive and defensive operations against Spain. Because of its special responsibilities for preserving the safety of England it was entitled to use torture in its investigations, the only body in the country so privileged. In April 1587 Andreas van Metter, a prisoner in the Tower, was accused of plotting against 'her Majesty's state and person', a charge 'which he did obstinately refuse to confess'. The Council thereupon ordered him to be subjected to 'the accustomed torture of the rack . . . to force him

[1] *APC* 1571–75, pp. 261–6; *APC* 1597–98, pp. 114–8.

to confess what might be had out of him'. The rack was not the only instrument of persuasion which councillors had at their disposal. In January 1599 Richard Denton and Peter Cooper were suspected of being 'privy unto some dangerous practice against the person of her Majesty and the state, as by some secret intelligence hath been already somewhat discovered'. They were committed 'to the prison of Bridewell . . . for the strict examination of them there . . ., using such means of torture by the manacles as . . . needful to make them . . . discover and declare the truth of the said practice'. Torture could also be employed in cases which posed a less direct threat to state security. It was used at the beginning of April 1583 upon one George Brown, who was suspected of murdering a London merchant. Poor Brown seems to have been unable to stand up to the treatment. In the middle of the same month the Council had to order the Lieutenant of the Tower, 'to send for a physician for George Brown to look unto him'.[1]

Busy as it was with public affairs the Council's work was made much more arduous by the attention which it was forced to devote to a great number of private petitions. In the year 1587 these included, among many others, requests from the University of Cambridge for the preservation of its privileges; from William Kelly, an Irish soldier, for a daily allowance as a reward for long and faithful service; from Anne Thickpenny, a grantee of Irish lands, for remission of rent; from the inhabitants of the liberty of Blackfriars in London for redress of 'certain inconveniences' within the liberty; and from William Davies against the Marshal of the Queen's Bench Prison.[2] Specific courts did exist to deal with such petitioners, but they pestered the Council, no doubt on the sound principle that if one wanted attention it was best to go as high as possible.

Consideration of these petitions took up a great deal of time. Indeed one piece of evidence for the general growth in the work of the Privy Council which certainly took place during the Elizabethan period is provided by its efforts to direct petitioners elsewhere. On 15 April 1582, 'considering what multitude of matters concerning private causes and actions between party and party were daily brought unto the Council Board, wherewith their

---

[1] *APC* 1587–88, p. 51; *APC* 1598–99, p. 428; *APC* 1571–75, pp. 92, 94, 96.
[2] *APC* 1587–88, *passim*.

Lordships were greatly troubled and her Majesty's special services oftentimes interrupted', the Council decided that, from then on:

no private causes arising between parties for any action whatsoever which may receive order and redress in any of her Majesty's ordinary courts shall be received and preferred to the Board, unless they shall concern the preservation of her Majesty's peace or shall be of some public consequence to touch the government of the realm.

This order seems to have had little effect, as, in October 1589, the councillors were 'continually so troubled and pestered with the said private suitors and their causes as at the times of their assembling for her Majesty's special services they can hardly be suffered . . . to attend and proceed in such causes as do concern her Majesty and the state of the realm'. Most of these suits still pertained to matters which had either been 'determined in other courts', or else 'ought to receive hearing and trial and order in the several courts . . . within the realm ordained for those purposes'. The councillors repeated their former prohibition against the bringing of such suits before the Council and also provided that:

if any suitors shall at any time hereafter resort either to her Majesty's principal secretary, or to the clerk or clerks of the Council . . ., or to the Council Board, as unacquainted with this order, whose causes shall manifestly appear to be of such kind as is aforesaid, that every such suitor and cause shall be addressed and directed either by her Majesty's principal secretary or in his absence from the Court by any two of the Council, or when the Council shall not be assembled then by one of the clerks of the Council . . ., either to the Lord Chancellor or masters of the Court of Requests (if the order thereof ought to be had in way of equity by course of those courts), or to such other courts of the common law or courts of equity or the courts for her Majesty's revenue where the said causes are properly determinable.

Even these elaborate provisions seem to have had little effect. In June 1591 the councillors stated that 'the multitude of private suitors' had lately increased because of 'some intermission of the due execution' of the instructions of October 1589, and commanded the masters of requests to see that their former decrees were put into effect.[1] There is no reason, however, to suppose

[1] *APC* 1581–82, pp. 394–5; *APC* 1589–90, pp. 181–2; *APC* 1591, p. 240.

that this last order was any more successful than its predecessors. There is no evidence of any significant decrease in the number of private suits brought before the Council after 1591.[1]

The increasing number of private suitors provides one illustration of the augmentation of the Council's work during the Elizabethan period. Another is the growing frequency of Council meetings. For most of the earlier part of the reign the rule was three meetings a week, on Tuesdays, Thursdays and Saturdays, either in the morning or in the afternoon, with special meetings when required.[2] Later, however, the Council met much oftener. In the 1590s there were meetings almost every day, including Sundays, sometimes both in the morning and in the afternoon.[3]

Why was there this significant increase in the Privy Council's work? One reason was clearly the growing importunities of private suitors. Another was the war with Spain, which occupied a good deal of the Council's time after 1585. A third was the dramatic increase which took place in the work of local government officials during the Elizabethan period. The Council had to supervise that work and its increased burdens were no doubt partly a reflection of the increased activities of the J.P.s in the localities.

The supervision of local officials, the consideration of private suits and the maintenance of orderly government involved the Council in judicial matters, yet it has recently been stated that, 'despite frequent statements to the contrary, and even though the sixteenth century liked to call all government institutions courts, the Elizabethan Privy Council was not a court in any real sense and had no judicial functions'.[4] This judgment seems too extreme. It may be true that, in the strictest technical sense, the Council was not a court, but to say that it did not exercise judicial functions seems to put an intolerable strain upon the evidence. It is true that it could not impose fines or order mutilation, but it could and did enforce its decisions in disputes between parties by arresting and imprisoning recalcitrant individuals until they yielded to its demands. This can be seen very clearly in a case between two Scottish merchants, Archibald and Edward Johnson,

---

[1] Cheyney, i, p. 74.
[2] *APC* 1558–70, pp. 267, 306; *APC* 1571–75, p. 180.
[3] Cheyney, i, p. 67.
[4] G. R. Elton, *The Tudor Constitution*, p. 101.

on the one hand, and a Norfolk gentleman, Roger Windham, on the other. One of the Johnsons' ships was wrecked on the coast of Norfolk in the late 1580s and Windham agreed to undertake 'the charge, safeguard and keeping' of the vessel and its goods. Despite this promise he allowed the Scots to be robbed of some of their property, whereupon the Council committed him to prison until he made restitution for the losses. Archibald Johnson, however, was not content. He pointed out that the Scottish Privy Council provided in such cases 'that the parties interested might have satisfaction of the goods and lands of those that were found faulty'. The councillors replied that they 'did afford . . . Johnson all the favour they could possibly', but that they 'had not any authority . . . by any law . . . to seize any lands and goods of any subject . . ., but yet their lordships had done what they might do in like cases, which was to commit . . . the party to prison, there to remain until he performed their order'. Windham was released for a time on bail, but the Council eventually instructed him to pay the Scots a sum of over £1,400 and imprisoned him again until he complied.[1] Windham would certainly have been surprised if he had been informed that the Council did not exercise judicial functions!

[1] *APC* 1590, pp. 380–82; *APC* 1590–91, pp. 149, 151; *APC* 1595–96, pp. 194–5, 248

CHAPTER THREE

Parliament

THE Queen and the Privy Council, the cogwheels of the Elizabethan government machine, worked continuously. Parliament,
in contrast, met occasionally and for short periods at a time.
During the entire reign of over forty-four years there were only
ten parliaments with a total of thirteen sessions. Moreover, sessions
averaged less than ten weeks in duration. The shortest, that of
1576, lasted four weeks and two days, the longest, in 1559,
fourteen weeks and six days, including ten days recess at Easter.[1]
There was, therefore, an average of more than three years between
each session, and Parliament was active for a period of less than
three years during the whole Elizabethan period.

These facts provide important clues about the Queen's
attitude towards Parliaments. It was the Queen alone who had
the right to summon, prorogue and dissolve them. The infrequency
and shortness of sessions suggest that for her they were necessary
evils. 'Her Majesty', Lord Keeper Sir John Puckering told
Parliament in 1593:

hath evermore been most loth to call for the assembly of her people in
Parliament and hath done the same but rarely and only upon most just,
weighty and great occasions. . . . Her Most Excellent Majesty would have
you all to know that . . ., of her own disposition, she would yet still
forbear, as she hath done, to draw you often together.[2]

By examining the 'weighty and great occasions' to which the
Lord Keeper referred we can discover the motives behind the
government's decision to summon Parliament.

[1] Neale, *Commons*, 381. One Parliament, that of 1572, had three sessions.
Another, that of 1563, had two. The rest had one each. A session was concluded
by either the prorogation or dissolution of the Parliament, prorogation when
the Queen decided to keep it in existence so that it could be assembled later for
another session, dissolution when she decided to bring it to an end.

[2] J. E. Neale, 'The Lord Keeper's Speech to the Parliament of 1592/3',
EHR, xxxi (1916), p. 130.

In 1559, when the first Parliament of the reign assembled, the reasons for its meeting were expounded by Lord Keeper Sir Nicholas Bacon. One great task, he said, was the 'well making of laws for ... uniting of the people of this realm into an uniform order of religion to the honour and glory of God, the establishment of His Church, and tranquility of the realm'. On a more mundane level, he stressed the need for money, but, he went on, the Queen, 'even from her own mouth', had commanded him to say that, 'were it not for the preservation of yourselves and the surety of the state, her Highness would have sooner adventured her life ... than she would have adventured to trouble her loving subjects' with requests for money.[1] The speech reflected the government's decision to introduce legislation to renew the breach with Rome and also its need for a subsidy following Mary's disastrous war with France which had resulted in the loss of Calais in 1558.

The need for legislation, the need for taxation: these themes recur again and again throughout the reign. The government's need for money explains the next two parliamentary sessions, those of 1563 and 1566. Elizabeth's intervention in Scotland in 1560 to aid the Protestant rebels there against the French dominated government of the Queen Regent, Mary of Guise, and her decision, in the autumn of 1562, to send troops across the channel to bolster up the Huguenot cause in the first of the French religious wars, necessitated heavy expenditure and consequently the need for taxation and a Parliament: hence the session of 1563. In spite of the grant of a subsidy at that time, however, the royal finances had still not recovered from the strains of the French expedition by 1566 when there had to be another session of Parliament and another request for a subsidy. It was granted, though this time there seems to have been some grumbling in the Commons at the government's demands.[2]

The next Parliament, that of 1571, met in the shadow of the Northern rebellion of 1569 and the Papal Bull of deposition, issued against the Queen in 1570. The government wished to put before it legislation to deal with the rebellion and counter the bull and also to ask for a subsidy: the cost of suppressing the revolt had been heavy. Sir Nicholas Bacon, in his oration at the opening

[1] Neale, *Parliaments*, i, pp. 42–3.
[2] *Ibid.*, pp. 85–6, 133, 137.

of the Parliament, divided his speech into two appropriate sections, law-making and supply. He passed quickly over the government's legislative programme and reserved most of his words for the subject of taxation, setting out the appeal for money after he had provided a glowing description of the benefits which the country had received from the Queen's rule: restoration of true religion; more than ten years of peace; the contrast between the condition of England and the state of her neighbours; clemency and mercy. Peace and clemency might have continued, he went on, but for the 'raging Romanist rebels'. The Commons' reaction on this occasion can be summed up in the words of their Speaker, who assured the Queen at the end of the session of 'the good will and hearty love the Lower House bare unto her', and added that they granted the subsidy without a single opposing voice.[1]

The next parliamentary session, that of 1572, was the first of the reign in which the government made no financial demands. It was summoned as a result of the discovery in the autumn of 1571 of the details of the Ridolphi Plot, a conspiracy involving rebellion, military aid from Alba in the Netherlands, the freeing of the captive Mary Queen of Scots and her marriage to the Duke of Norfolk, the restoration of Catholicism in England, and doubtless the death of Elizabeth as well. The plot showed the desirability of devising laws for the Queen's safety and this was the reason, 'so necessary and so weighty' as Lord Keeper Bacon put it, for the calling of Parliament. The measure which Lords and Commons thought most necessary for the protection of the Queen, a violent bill against Mary Queen of Scots, was, however, too strong for Elizabeth to stomach. She vetoed it.[2] Parliament was prorogued and the Queen did not summon it again until she had urgent need for money. When it did assemble in 1576 Sir Walter Mildmay, the Chancellor of the Exchequer, a man who seems to have been a clear and effective speaker, put the royal request before the Commons. He enumerated various special causes of expenditure which the last parliamentary grant had been insufficient to cover and took pains to lay stress on the Queen's personal frugality, pointing out that she lived without excess, 'either in building or in other superfluous things of pleasure'. The subsidy was granted without difficulty, rather surprisingly,

---

[1] *Ibid.*, pp. 178, 186–7, 237.
[2] *Ibid.*, pp. 241, 244, 309–10.

perhaps, in view of the fact that the country was at peace. It may be that by this time the idea of parliamentary taxation as an extraordinary source of revenue, appropriate only in wartime, was beginning to wear a little thin.[1]

Money was demanded again in 1581, when the Parliament of 1572 met for its third and final session. On this occasion, however, the need for taxation was coupled with the need for legislation against the Catholic threat which had become especially acute in 1580 with the beginnings of the Jesuit mission to England. Mildmay dealt at some length with this menace when he set the government's programme before the Commons. The Pope, he said, had emboldened many undutiful subjects 'to stand fast in their disobedience to her Majesty and her laws. . . . The obstinate and stiff-necked Papist is so far from being reformed as he hath gotten stomach to go backwards and to show his disobedience, not only in arrogant words but also in contemptuous deeds.' In order to encourage such attitudes the Pope had recently

sent hither a sort of hypocrites, naming themselves Jesuits, a rabble of vagrant friars newly sprung up and coming through the world to trouble the Church of God; whose principal errand is, by creeping into the houses and familiarities of men of behaviour and reputation, not only to corrupt the realm with false doctrine, but also, under that pretence, to stir sedition.

As for remedies, Mildmay, having remarked on the Queen's previous 'gentle manner of dealing' with Catholics, suggested that it was time 'to look more narrowly and straitly to them, lest ... they prove dangerous members ... in the entrails of our Commonwealth'. In short, severer laws against them were necessary. Another requirement was the provision of sufficient forces to meet any threat either at home or abroad. This, Mildmay hastened to point out, involved great expenses. In other words. taxation was necessary. It was a stirring speech which clearly appealed to the strongly Protestant and fanatically patriotic Commons. The ultimate outcome was the grant of a subsidy and the passing of an 'Act to retain the Queen's Majesty's subjects in their due obedience' – the rigorous law which marked the start of the severest persecution of Catholics which took place during the Elizabethan period.[2]

[1] *Ibid.*, pp. 348–9.
[2] *Ibid*, pp. 383–4, 386.

The next Parliament, that of 1584, was called in an atmosphere of crisis. The previous year Walsingham's diligence had uncovered the Throckmorton plot, a widespread conspiracy which aimed at the murder of Elizabeth and her replacement by Mary Queen of Scots. Then, in the summer of 1584, William of Orange, the main champion of European Protestantism next to Elizabeth herself, was assassinated by a fanatic. The government realized the need for new legislation to protect the Queen, and the main business of the session was an act for the Queen's safety. As finally passed this provided for the death penalty for any person who was concerned in a plot against Elizabeth's life and throne. It thus served as a legal basis for the execution of Mary Queen of Scots in 1587. The other important legislative measure of the Parliament, an act against Jesuits and seminary priests, sought to destroy the foundation of the Catholic mission by ordering all priests ordained abroad to leave the country within forty days or else suffer the penalty of traitors. The government also asked for money. Mildmay, in his speech for supply, pointed out that Ireland alone had consumed, since the last Parliament, more than the entire grant which had then been made. Moreover, elaborate provisions had recently been necessary to defend England against possible attack. Great quantities of powder and munitions had been bought, 'the mass whereof is more than in any former time'. Then there was 'the new building and repairing of the navy, put now in better strength and better readiness than at any time before this: a matter of great importance, for the navy, being justly termed the wall of England, is a thing of all other principally to be cared for.' No Elizabethan House of Commons could refuse an appeal couched in these terms. A subsidy was granted.[1]

The following Parliament, which met in 1586, was not summoned to make laws or vote money. The Lord Chancellor, Sir Thomas Bromley, made that quite clear in his opening speech. The purpose of the meeting was 'rare and extraordinary, of great weight, great peril, and dangerous consequence'. It was, in fact, to consider the position of Mary Queen of Scots following clear proof of her involvement in the Babington Conspiracy of 1586. Parliament had no doubt about the fate she deserved: execution. Its pressure upon the Queen, joined to that of the Privy Council was the main reason behind Elizabeth's decision

[1] Neale, *Parliaments*, ii, pp. 37, 51, 53, 54–6.

to publish the formal sentence of death which had already been passed upon Mary, a decision which was an important stage in the series of events leading to the beheading of the Scottish Queen in February 1587.[1]

Parliament's next meeting, in 1589, took place in a very different atmosphere. The country and the government were still rejoicing at the famous victory of the previous year over the Spanish Armada. This sense of euphoria did not, however, lessen the preoccupation of Queen and Council with the financial problem. The expenses involved in defeating the Spanish fleet and putting the country in a state of readiness against invasion had been very heavy. When Parliament met, the Lord Chancellor, Sir Christopher Hatton, in a powerful opening oration, stressed the continuing threat from Spain. 'Our enemies make great preparation to assail us by sea,' he said 'our navy must be made fit to encounter them. They have great strength to invade us by land: a correspondency of force must be had to withstand them. . . . Our duties towards God, her Majesty and our country doth require all this at your hands.' Hatton's carefully prepared speech provided the background for the extraordinary request which the government was about to lay before the Commons: an appeal for a double subsidy. There seems to have been some grumbling at this unprecedented demand, but little real trouble; the Commons were too patriotic for that.[2]

The war against Spain, which had started with the English expedition of 1585 to the Netherlands, continued with ever mounting costs during the 1590s and the last three Parliaments of the reign were summoned specifically to make large financial grants. In 1593, however, the government also had legislation in mind. In spite of the laws of 1581 and 1584 Catholic priests remained at work in the country, strengthening the faith of wavering members of their flock and making new converts as well. Hence the government's two bills – both to be substantially altered in their passage through Parliament – which sought to stamp out recusancy by providing for drastic measures against rank and file Catholics. At least as important as these religious bills, in the eyes of Queen and Council at any rate, was the need for money. In 1593 Elizabeth was engaged in helping the French King, Henry IV,

[1] *Ibid.*, pp. 106, 133.
[2] *Ibid.*, pp. 193, 201, 205–7.

against the forces of the Catholic League. The cost of keeping an army in France and providing Henry with subsidies, when added to the continuing expense of operations in the Netherlands, imposed an enormous financial burden on the Crown, a burden far greater than Elizabeth could bear without substantial parliamentary assistance. In this situation the Commons agreed to provide two subsidies. The Lords did not think that this was enough and asked for three, a remarkable attack on the well established prescriptive right of the Commons to initiate taxation. Three subsidies were clearly necessary, however, in view of the Crown's parlous financial situation and the Commons finally agreed, though not before they had indulged in a good deal of wrangling with the Upper House.[1]

This triple subsidy did not last long. The final payment was due early in 1597 and the continuance of war meant that the government could not delay in seeking further financial aid. Parliament, therefore, was summoned for October 1597. The Lord Keeper, Sir Thomas Egerton, in his opening speech, stressed the exceptional nature of the struggle with Spain, which was being fought, not as previous wars had been, 'either of ambition to enlarge dominions, or of revenge to quit injuries', but because 'the holy religion of God is sought to be rooted out, the whole realm to be subdued, and the precious life of her excellent Majesty to be taken away'. The Queen had 'not spared to disburse a mass of treasure and to sell her land for maintenance of her armies by sea and land'. Despite this, he went on, taxation was essential. Anyone who was unwilling to contribute was very foolish.

He that would seek to lay up treasure and so enrich himself, should be like to him that would busy himself to beautify his house when the city where he dwelleth were on fire, or to deck up his cabin when the ship wherein he saileth were ready to drown. ... To give is to give to ourselves.

This was a prelude to the government's request for three subsidies, a demand which seems to have met with no opposition, though there was some unsuccessful resistance to the suggestion that all three should be collected in three years and not spread over four, as the three subsidies of 1593 had been.[2]

Despite the triple subsidies of 1593 and 1597 the government's

[1] *Ibid.*, pp. 241, 280, 281, 296, 299–310.
[2] *Ibid.*, 325, 327-8, 360–61.

financial position was desperate when Parliament met once more in October 1601. The Earl of Essex had spent money like water on his Irish expedition of 1599 but had still failed to crush the rebellion there. To make matters worse the Spaniards had landed an army at Kinsale on the south coat of Ireland in September 1601, a threat which demanded immediate and expensive action. Sir Robert Cecil emphasized the seriousness of the situation in a speech to the House of Commons at the beginning of November. In Ireland, he said, 'we have . . . an army, and nothing but an army; fed, even, out of England'. The Queen 'selleth her land to defend us. . . . What we freely give unto her she living bestows it to our good, and dying doubtless will leave it for our profit'. The government asked for and got four subsidies.[1]

In the above analysis Parliament has avowedly been studied from the government's point of view. Sir John Neale has demonstrated in unforgettable prose that the ordinary M.P.s, those representatives of the gentry class who filled the Elizabethan House of Commons, regarded Parliaments as occasions when they could discuss the great questions of the day, questions such as religion and the succession to the throne. The government's attitude was clearly very different. On only one occasion was Parliament specifically summoned to consider a major political issue: that was in 1586 when it was asked to discuss the position of Mary Queen of Scots. In no fewer than eleven out of the thirteen sessions of Elizabethan Parliaments the government asked for money; one subsidy or more on each occasion. In six out of the thirteen sessions it had important legislation to put before Parliament. In other words, from the government's point of view Parliament was essentially an assembly for granting taxes and passing laws, with the emphasis on the former function.

Subsidy bills and other important public enactments would, however, have passed less smoothly than they did if the government had not been very conscious of the need for effective management of Parliament, especially of the House of Commons. It used to be thought that the Crown exercised control over the Lower House by interfering in elections. This view was expressed in its most extreme form by Canon Dixon, who wrote in 1902, 'No Tudor House of Commons but was packed'.[2] We now know that

[1] *Ibid.* 370, 411–5.
[2] R. W. Dixon, *History of the Church of England*, V (Oxford, 1902), p. 54.

this thesis is quite untenable. One piece of evidence which has been put forward in its support, the creation during the Tudor period of large numbers of new borough seats – sixty-two in the reign of Elizabeth alone – was not in fact an illustration of the government's determination to pack the Commons; it was rather the result of pressure brought to bear upon the Crown by important borough patrons, eminent men like the Elizabethan Earls of Leicester, Huntingdon and Rutland. They in their turn were being subjected to the demands of the country gentlemen who invaded the borough seats in ever increasing numbers as the Tudor period progressed. It was perfectly natural that peers and leading courtiers should seek to satisfy this growing clamour of the local gentry for parliamentary seats, either by getting them returned for existing boroughs or by persuading the Queen to create new seats. It was all part and parcel of the Elizabethan clientage system. The gentry got the seats they wanted, and the courtiers or peers who acted as their patrons got additional loyal supporters.

It seems quite certain that the Queen and Council did not employ crude electoral methods to secure the return of favoured M.P.s. The great majority of the Court group of officials and gentlemen servants of the greatest figures of the realm – a group which accounted for between a quarter and a fifth of the total membership of the Commons during the later Parliaments of the reign – secured their seats, like so many of their colleagues among the country gentry, as a result of the personal backing of peers and courtiers, not as a consequence of any deliberate government policy.[1] Elizabethan Parliaments were not packed, though to say that is not to deny the importance from the government's point of view of the powerful nucleus of officials who sat in every House of Commons during the period. These men gained their seats through the normal workings of the patronage system, but the Crown could usually depend upon their loyal support.

One of the Queen's greatest weapons in the management of Parliament was undoubtedly her own personality. She sometimes intervened directly, taking action to stay matters which she disliked. In 1563 a bill was introduced in the Commons 'for allowance to sheriffs upon their accounts for justices' diets'. It was a

[1] Neale, *Commons*, pp. 140–41, 146, 152, 288–98.

minor enough matter in itself, but in Elizabeth's eyes it represented a parliamentary attempt to encroach by statute on the
sphere of administration, that is to say on matters which properly
belonged to the royal prerogative. She consequently sent messages
to both the Lords and the Commons, informing them that she
'would take order therein herself'. We hear no more about the
bill. Another occasion on which the Queen intervened, this time
in a very much more important affair, was in 1587, when Anthony
Cope laid before the Commons the notorious bill and book in
which he attempted to sweep away the entire existing structure of the Church of England. Elizabeth, who considered all
ecclesiastical measures to be matters for the Crown rather than for
the Commons, acted at once. She sent for the bill and book and,
having perused them, 'commanded no more should be said' in
the matter.[1] These are only two examples among many which
could be cited, but they do illustrate how the Queen was determined to preserve the rights of her prerogative. The Commons
did not always submit readily to her commands, but the combination of tact and firmness which she habitually employed usually
enabled her to get her way.

Another method of control employed by the Queen was the
use of her power of veto. In all she vetoed sixty-six or sixty-seven
bills during the course of her reign, an average of just over five
for each parliamentary session. The largest number rejected at
any one time was fifteen in 1585; the smallest, one in each of the
sessions of 1559, 1581 and 1593. The principles on which Elizabeth worked seem clear. She vetoed bills which she had not had
time to examine properly as well as those which she disliked.[2]

A third and very drastic means of keeping Parliament in line,
but one which the Queen did not hesitate to employ, was the
imprisonment of unduly obstreperous members of the House of
Commons. During the Parliament of 1586–87 Peter Wentworth,
Anthony Cope, Edward Lewkenor, Ranulf Hurleston and Robert
Bainbridge were all sent to the Tower for discussing Cope's bill
and book outside Parliament. This was an offence not protected
by privilege and they seem to have remained in prison until the
end of the session. In 1593 Wentworth was in trouble again, this

[1] Neale, *Parliaments*, i, 121–2; ii, 148. 152, 157.

[2] *Ibid.*, i, 82, 128, 171, 240, 310, 363, 415; ii, 98, 190, 239, 323, 367,
427.

time as the central figure in a plot to introduce a bill on the succession. He and his accomplices discussed the matter outside the Commons and consequently four of them were arrested, including Wentworth himself, who was sent to the Tower where he remained until his death in 1597. During this same Parliament the Queen took stern measures against three other members who aroused her displeasure: two were imprisoned and the other was forbidden to appear in the Commons. None of these actions was unconstitutional but taken together they were a crude reminder of the realities of royal power at a time when the Queen's temper may have been becoming less equable with the approach of old age.[1]

The imprisonment of members; the use of the royal veto; interventions to stay bills: these were three ways in which the Queen sought to control the work of Parliament. This, however, is only one half of the story. The essence of Elizabeth's skill lay in the charm which she exercised, in the *rapport* which she was usually able to establish with her Parliaments. The best evidence of this is to be found in her speeches and messages to the two Houses and in the reaction of the Lords and Commons, especially the Commons, to them. One striking example of her skill can be drawn from the Parliament of 1584. On 19 December she sent a message to the Commons informing them that she intended to adjourn Parliament over Christmas so that members could return home 'for their better ease and recreation'. The message was most graciously worded and the Commons resolved to return, through their councillor-members, their humble gratitude for her good opinion of them. This gave Elizabeth an opportunity to raise their affection to a still greater pitch. She sent another message with her 'most hearty and loving thanks . . ., redoubling to them their thanks ten-thousand-thousand fold', and ascribed the long peace and prosperity which God had bestowed upon the country to the merits 'of so religious, godly and obedient subjects'. We cannot measure, only imagine, the extent to which such words rendered the Commons amenable to the royal wishes. Even in her later years the Queen was still capable of producing the old Elizabethan enchantments. The Parliament of 1593 was, as already noted, a troublesome one. Seven members of the Lower House were imprisoned or sequestered during its course. Yet the

[1] Neale, *Parliaments*, ii, 157, 165, 256–60, 265, 275–8.

Queen's closing speech to the assembled Lords and Commons was one of her finest efforts. 'Many wiser princes than myself you have had,' she told them,

> but, one only excepted [Henry VIII] – whom in the duty of a child I must regard, and to whom I must acknowledge myself far shallow – I may truly say, none whose love and care can be greater, or whose desire can be more to fathom deeper for prevention of danger to come, or resisting of dangers if attempted towards you, shall ever be found to exceed myself.

She concluded by thanking Parliament for the subsidy bill.[1]

The giving of the royal assent to the next subsidy bill, that of 1597, was used by the Queen to make one of those dramatic gestures in which she delighted. As the Clerk of the Parliaments intoned the royal assent in the traditional form,'*La Royne remercie ses loyaulx subjects, accepte leur benevolence, et aussi le veult*', Elizabeth 'rose up and bended herself to the commonalty, opening her arms and hands; and then the commonalty kneeled, and then she sat down and they stood up again'. It was a charming gesture, a perfect illustration of that personal magic which Elizabeth had used throughout the years to get her way with Parliaments. The magic was wearing somewhat thin in the 1590s, as we shall see, but the Queen could still sometimes conjure it up for a great occasion.[2]

Like the Queen, privy councillors played an important part in the management of Parliament. Indeed, one of the main themes of a famous lecture[3] is the ability with which councillors ordered and arranged Commons business in the Elizabethan period and the passing of such skilful guidance under the early Stuarts. It was one of the duties of councillors to introduce important government bills and to steer them as smoothly as possible through Parliament. They seem generally to have managed this with great skill during Elizabeth's reign, though they did not hesitate, on occasion, to take stern measures to get their way. In 1593, for example, a government bill against sectaries was much criticized by a House of Commons which still had strong Puritan

1 *Ibid.*, 42, 321–2.

2 Neale, *Commons*, 425.

3 W. Notestein, *The Winning of the Initiative by the House of Commons* (British Academy Raleigh Lecture in History, 1924).

sympathies. At the report stage, after the second reading, the critics were still dissatisfied, despite the drastic amendments which had already been made and called for further amendments and for the bill to be committed once more. 'The Council', a contemporary diarist tells us, were 'much against' this, as Parliament was near its end and further elaborate discussion would put the bill in jeopardy. Finally, at the suggestion of Sir Robert Cecil, the doors of the House were closed, while a committee went to the Lords to add further amendments and bring the bill back for a third reading in the Commons. As a result, the House was kept in session until three in the afternoon, though the normal time of rising was about noon. 'We were content to yield to anything, so we might rise,' wrote one member, a sufficient commentary on the success of the Council's stratagem.[1]

Discussion of the committee system also throws light on the Council's methods of managing the Commons. Bills were normally referred, after the second reading, to committees, where detailed debate took place, and it is very noticeable that privy councillors were named on every committee. Indeed, when a committee was for an important measure the list of members was headed by 'all the Privy Council of the House of Commons'. Moreover, it was often a councillor who laid the committee's report before the House, especially if the bill was an important one. The detailed knowledge which councillors had of the issues behind most bills and the authority which their office gave them must have made them formidable figures on committees. This seems to have been especially true of the earlier part of the reign, when the committee system certainly helped to maintain the dominance of the Privy Council in the House. In later years its advantage from the government's point of view was more questionable.[2]

Councillors were also powers to be reckoned with in the conduct of everyday business on the floor of the Commons, making numerous speeches and generally influencing the course of debates. The seats which they occupied were those immediately adjacent to the Speaker's chair, and this gave them the opportunity, when need arose, to whisper advice in his ear. On one occasion during the 1601 parliament, 'Mr. Secretary Cecil ... spake something in Mr. Speaker's ear'. Soon after the Speaker rose and

[1] Notestein, 15; Neale, *Commons*, 402–3.
[2] Notestein, 18–20, 23.

closed the sitting without fulfilling a previous promise to let a member read a bill against monopolies.[1]

Co-operation between Speaker and privy councillors was, indeed, one of the features of the Elizabethan House of Commons. The Speaker was theoretically elected at the beginning of each Parliament by the whole House on the nomination of the senior privy councillor present. In practice the government had decided beforehand who he was to be, and the 'election' was little more than a formality. Sir Edward Coke, who was 'named to be Speaker ... at Hampton Court' by the Queen and Council on 28 January 1593 and was 'elected' by the Commons on 19 February, later declared that the practice was for the sovereign to 'name a discreet and learned man whom the Commons elect'. The fact that the Speaker was a government appointee, amenable to the directions of Queen and Council, was very important, as he exercised considerable control over Commons procedure, usually determining the order in which bills were read. As a result measures in which the government was interested were usually favoured.[2]

So far, in this account of parliamentary management, the House of Lords has been well in the background. This is partly because of lack of evidence. Elizabethan peers, unlike their contemporaries in the Commons, do not seem to have kept parliamentary diaries. It is clear, however, that the Upper House was much more subservient to the Crown than the Lower. Government measures which were likely to meet with difficulty in the Commons were frequently introduced in the Upper House – the 1593 bill against sectaries, mentioned above, is an example – and it was always open to the Lords to reject Commons bills which met with government disapproval, as in 1589 when they refused to read two bills touching the prerogative which the Commons had sent up with special recommendations.[3]

It is right to note the skill with which Elizabeth used the House of Lords, the Speaker and the Privy Council to influence and restrain the Commons and thus manage in her own interests, the business of Parliament. It is also necessary, however, to realize that by the last decade of the reign significant changes were

---

[1] Notestein, 20–21; Neale, *Commons*, 364–5.
[2] Neale, *Commons*, 354–5, 393–7.
[3] Notestein, 24; Neale, *Parliaments*, ii, 210–11.

taking place in the relationship between Crown and Commons, changes which pointed the way towards the developments of the Stuart period.

The general parliamentary atmosphere of Elizabeth's last years seems to have been one of growing turbulence. The 1593 House of Commons was not notable for the calmness of its proceedings and by the turn of the century things had got much worse. 'I have been . . . a member of this House in six or seven Parliaments, yet never did I see the House in so great confusion', said Sir Robert Cecil in 1601, referring to the great Commons debate of that year on monopolies. Members had been shouted down during the discussion. This, as Cecil put it, was 'more fit for a grammar school than a court of Parliament'. The growing truculence of M.P.s may have been due partly to outside influences; parliamentary business was being openly discussed in the streets in 1601, a scandalous thing in the eyes of contemporary statesmen. It was a shocked and disgusted Cecil who told the House, 'I have heard myself, being in my coach, these words spoken aloud: "God prosper those that further the overthrow of . . . monopolies. God send the prerogative touch not our liberty."' [1]

The growing turmoil within Parliament was also partly due to the slackening grip of the government on the House of Commons. The great councillors who had set the tone of leadership in the early and high Elizabethan periods, men like Knollys, Sadler, Hatton and Mildmay, were dead or senile by 1593. They did have a noteworthy successor in Sir Robert Cecil, but he was only one man, and the other councillor-members of the House were mediocrities. It was during these years, too, that the committee system, which had previously aided councillors so much in their efforts to control the Commons, became at least as much a liability as an asset to them. By the 1590s committees were filching from councillors much of the work of drawing up legislation and were beginning to take initiatives on questions of general policy, such as vagrancy, poverty and enclosures. This was the start of a tendency which was to culminate in disaster for the Crown, in the early Stuart period, when private members, working largely through the committee system, succeeded in wresting control of the Commons from the government. [2]

[1] Notestein, 22; Neale, *Parliaments*, ii, 384, 386.
[2] Neale, *Parliaments*, ii, 343–4; Notestein, 23.

Above all, however, it was the government's financial situation in the 1590s which made it possible for the members of the Commons to make their voices heard in no uncertain terms. In ten sessions of Parliament from 1559 to 1589 the Crown asked for a total of nine subsidies. In three sessions between 1593 and 1601, plagued by the ever mounting costs of the war with Spain, it asked for ten. In these years the Commons were increasingly 'paying the piper'. It is hardly surprising that they also tried more and more to 'call the tune'. Their frontal assault on the prerogative in the monopolies debate of 1601 showed how far they were prepared to go. The Queen succeeded, on that occasion, in preserving the form of her prerogative rights only by conceding the substance of the Commons' demands. It was a hollow victory.

In these last years of Elizabeth's life there does seem to have been, at times, a real lack of warmth in the relations between Queen and Commons. This is certainly suggested by an episode which took place in 1601 at the end of the ceremony at which Elizabeth confirmed the Commons' choice of a Speaker. As she left the Upper House and passed through the members of the Commons gathered at the bar of the Lords' chamber:

few said, 'God bless your Majesty', as they were wont in all great assemblies. And the throng being great and little room to pass she moved her hand to have more room, whereupon one of the gentlemen ushers said openly, 'back masters, make room'. And one answered stoutly behind, 'if you will hang us we can make no more room,' which the Queen seemed not to hear, though she heaved up her head and looked that way towards him that spake.[1]

This was a different atmosphere from the ecstacies of the high Elizabethan period, when the relations between Queen and Commons had the air of a great romance.

[1] H. Townshend, *Historical Collections* (1680), 178–9.

CHAPTER FOUR

The Central Administration

MEMBERS of the Elizabethan ruling classes would have agreed about the basic objectives of government: to keep law and order within the realm and punish disturbers of the Queen's peace; to defend the country against foreign powers; to raise enough money to ensure the administration and defence of the realm; and to take a paternalistic interest in the welfare of the subject. The officials of local government and of the central administration working together under the direction of the sovereign and the Privy Council existed to secure these objectives. Local institutions will claim attention later; here we are concerned with the central machinery and its development during the Elizabethan period.

Many organs of central government were concerned with the preservation of law and order and the punishment of evil-doers, a reflection both of the intrinsic importance of the task and of the overwhelming contemporary emphasis – inherited from the middle ages – on the role of the sovereign as the dispenser of justice. Some of these institutions, the Exchequer and Chancery for instance, performed both administrative and judicial functions on a large scale, but even those courts which did not undertake elaborate administrative as well as judicial tasks – for example the courts of King's Bench, Common Pleas, Requests and Star Chamber – must have their places in any account of Tudor central government. By serving the ends of justice they were performing one of the primary tasks for which the Elizabethan administration existed.

The law of England, the 'common law' of the realm, rooted in ancient custom which had been modified and developed by the legislation of kings and parliaments and by judicial decisions was administered in three central courts, King's Bench, Common Pleas and Exchequer. Originally King's Bench was concerned with pleas of the Crown, matters in which the King was concerned – which meant principally criminal cases of all kinds;

Common Pleas was responsible for suits between subjects; and the Exchequer was concerned with revenue cases. By the Elizabethan period, however, this division of functions had broken down. By then both King's Bench and Exchequer had breached Common Pleas' monopoly of cases between subjects, a feat which they were able to accomplish by offering better remedies and speedier procedures than were available in Common Pleas.[1]

These 'better remedies' and 'speedier procedures' were, however, entirely relative and by the sixteenth century the whole common law system, as expressed in the three central courts, displayed serious deficiencies. These have been well summarized by Dr. Elton in the statement that 'common-law procedure in civil cases tended to deprive [the] plaintiff of a remedy; in criminal cases it handicapped the Crown.'[2] Fortunately, however, both Crown and subject could seek remedies in places other than the three ancient common law courts. One of the most important of these was Star Chamber, the King's Council sitting as a court. Its authority did not derive from statute but rested upon the traditional authority of the Council to redress grievances. From 1540 onwards, at the latest, the Privy Council and Star Chamber were entirely separate institutions, each served by its own clerical staff, but their personnel was the same, except that the chief justices of King's Bench and Common Pleas sat with the privy councillors as judges in the Court of Star Chamber.

The scope of Star Chamber's work was limited by its inability to deprive the subject of life or property. This meant in practice, that it could not deal with cases of treason and felony which might involve the loss of both. It did concern itself with breaches of public order. This was its original and remained its chief task, but it also supervised and protected the enforcement of the law in the other courts of the realm and adjudicated on violations of royal proclamations. During Elizabeth's reign the court met twice a week in term time, on Wednesdays and Fridays. Sessions usually began at 9 in the morning and closed at 11 a.m. They were held in public. Cases were started by bills of complaint which were brought by the attorney-general in the case of public prosecutions and in other suits by a private attorney, and punishments for

[1] On these courts and their development see W. S. Holdsworth, *History of English Law*, i, (7th ed. 1956), p. 194ff.
[2] G. R. Elton, *The Tudor Constitution*, p. 150.

guilty parties usually took the form of fines. Procedure, which followed the pattern of the courts of equity, was swift and simple – at least compared with that of the common law courts. During Elizabeth's reign more than 30,000 cases came before it. Its evident popularity, a reflection no doubt of the eminence of its membership as well as of the relative efficiency and speed of its procedure, seems to have continued throughout the whole of the Queen's reign, unaffected by the growing severity of punishments during her later years.[1]

The criminal jurisdiction of Star Chamber clearly helped to fill the gap left in the legal system by the deficiences of the common law. So too in civil jurisdiction did the Court of Chancery. The judicial functions of Chancery reflected the duty of the sovereign to see that right was done to all subjects. Such right could often be denied by the common law courts, with their rigid, formalized procedures. Chancery on the other hand, applied principles of equity, that is to say of common sense and fairness, to legal problems. It is true that during the sixteenth century equity procedure began to acquire formality and definition, but in Elizabeth's reign the court was still a more flexible instrument of justice than the common law courts.

Chancery, however, was much more than a court of equity. It also possessed a common law jurisdiction, and it was a secretariat which wrote, sealed and recorded all instruments dispatched under the Great Seal. That seal was used not only to authenticate all royal grants but was also necessary on all original writs (writs starting legal actions), and was the seal employed by Star Chamber. The administrative duties of Chancery – and those cited above were merely the most important – together with its judicial work made it one of the largest departments of state. We must be wary of attempting to make precise distinctions between its administrative and judicial work. The common law jurisdiction of the Lord Chancellor arose directly from the court's administrative duties: the great majority of common law cases heard in Chancery arose from instruments enrolled there. Moreover, holders of individual Chancery offices usually dealt with both judicial and administrative work. Such a mixing of administrative and judicial functions does not necessarily preclude efficiency, but the sixteenth century saw a vast increase in the quantity of

[1] G. R. Elton, *The Tudor Constitution*, p. 158ff; Cheyney, i, p. 81ff.

Chancery's work and the result seems to have been far from happy. Dr. Jones in his study of the Elizabethan Chancery paints a picture of multiplication of personnel, confusion of duties and delay in enrolments. Before the important reforms by Lord Keeper Egerton in the 1590s Chancery was certainly an 'administrative mess'. In these circumstances the relative flexibility of its judicial procedure must often have seemed of doubtful value to litigants caught up in the complications of Chancery administration.[1]

Chancery, however, was not the only refuge available for those unable to obtain remedy at common law. There was also the Court of Requests. This had a continuous existence dating from the later fifteenth century and was designed in theory for suitors who desired equitable remedy for their legal problems but were prevented from suing in Chancery because of poverty or the trivial nature of their complaints. In fact it is very difficult to make any distinction at all between cases heard in the courts of Requests and Chancery. The majority of suitors in Requests seem to have been more concerned with having their grievances heard in a court of equity than with being excused the payment of fees – a privilege to which they were entitled if they were admitted to plead as paupers. There is, however, no evidence that Chancery felt any jealousy of the lesser court's engrossing cases which might equally properly have come before itself. In an age of greatly increasing litigation there was more than enough work to keep both courts busy.

The work of the Court of Requests was sufficiently effective to draw down upon it the wrath of the common lawyers and by the end of the reign it found itself in a most unsatisfactory position, the legality of its whole jurisidiction having been challenged by the Court of Common Pleas.[2] This conflict, however, was only one facet of a wider movement on the part of the common law courts in general and the Court of Common Pleas in particular to restrict the jurisdiction of courts which followed procedures different from their own. This can be seen in the disputes which came to the fore at the end of the reign – and especially from the

[1] The only satisfactory study of the Elizabethan Chancery is by W. J. Jones, 'The Elizabethan Chancery: some legal and other aspects', (London University Ph.D. thesis, 1958).

[2] W. B. J. Allsebrook, 'The Court of Requests in the Reign of Elizabeth', (London University M.A. thesis, 1936), pp. 110–16, 150–61.

1590s onwards – between the common law on the one hand and the equitable, prerogative and civil law jurisdictions of the Councils of the North and in the Marches of Wales and the Court of Admiralty on the other.[1] Here was a foreshadowing of the struggle between prerogative courts and common lawyers which was to play such an important part in the constitutional history of the early seventeenth century.

The Councils of the North and in the Marches of Wales were, of course, more than courts of law. They had very wide administrative as well as judicial powers and were essentially instruments for applying the will of the central government in the more remote and lawless parts of the realm. The Council in the Marches, which originated in the later fifteenth century but developed as a formal conciliar court only in the 1530s, exercised jurisdiction in the Elizabethan period over the twelve Welsh shires, together with the counties of Monmouth, Hereford, Gloucester, Worcester, Shropshire and, until 1569, Cheshire. It had very wide judicial powers, trying criminal cases which involved capital offences as well as misdemeanours and, in addition, exercising an extensive civil jurisdiction. In trying cases of treason, murder and felony the court observed the normal procedures of common law, but in dealing with lesser crimes and in civil cases it followed the prerogative and equitable methods of Star Chamber and Chancery. In addition, there were its administrative tasks: especially important here were the wide police and military powers which it exercised throughout its jurisdiction. In these contexts the suppression of recusancy and the need to guard against the possibility of foreign invasion added substantially to the Council's burdens during the Elizabethan period.[2] The Council was, in fact, in the words of its most recent historian, 'responsible for almost every aspect of life in Wales and the border'.[3] At times, under the presidency or direction of able men, it seems to have worked well. At other times, and notably in the 1590s, it was comparatively ineffective.[4]

[1] R. R. Reid, *The King's Council in the North* (1921), p. 343ff; P. Williams, *The Council in the Marches of Wales under Elizabeth I* (Cardiff, 1958), p. 225; Cheyney, i, p. 121ff.

[2] P. Williams, *The Council in the Marches of Wales under Elizabeth I*, 6–33, 65–83, 85–126.

[3] *Ibid.*, 312.

[4] *Ibid.*, 316.

The origin and powers of the Council of the North were similar to those of the Council in the Marches. Its history can be traced back to Yorkist times, but it took permanent form in the 1530s. From then on, and throughout the reign of Elizabeth, it was the body which the government employed to impose its will on the northern parts of the realm. With its wide administrative and judicial powers it had some measure of success, especially during the presidency of the third Earl of Huntingdon, whose twenty-three year tenure of office ended in 1595.[1]

The preservation of law and order in England, the task of the central and regional courts and councils under the ever watchful eye of the Privy Council, was also peculiarly the responsibility of one of the most important figures in the Elizabethan administrative structure, the principal secretary.[2] Until the reign of Henry VIII the secretary was merely the king's personal servant, in charge of his private correspondence, and not in the first rank of officers of state. The change came with Thomas Cromwell, secretary from 1534 to 1540 and the first layman to hold the office. Cromwell used his position as the King's chief adviser to give the secretary a hold on almost all the affairs of the realm. After his death the office was often divided between two holders, but although its standing dropped for a time, its potentialities were fully exploited again in Elizabeth's reign by the two Cecils and Walsingham, who made it a key office in the state. Their tenure of the post spanned almost the entire reign, Burghley being secretary from 1558 to 1572, Walsingham from 1573 to 1590, and Robert Cecil from 1596 to 1612, and it is important to note that it was the men who made the office, not the office the men. In other words, it was because Walsingham and the Cecils were intrinsically such able and important ministers that they raised the office of secretary to the heights which it had achieved by the end of the century. Just what these heights were can perhaps best be seen by reading the words of Robert Cecil, who himself wrote an account of the secretary's position. 'All officers and counsellors of princes,' Cecil affirmed, 'have a prescribed authority by patent, by custom, or by oath, the secretary only excepted.' The secretary, in contrast, had.

[1] R. R. Reid, *The King's Council in the North*, p. 41ff, p. 209ff.

[2] For the development of the office until the end of the sixteenth century see F. M. G. Evans, *The Principal Secretary of State* (Manchester, 1923), pp. 10–60.

a liberty to negotiate at discretion at home and abroad, with friends and enemies, all matters of speech and intelligence. . . . As long as any matter of what weight soever, is handled only between the prince and the secretary, those counsels are compared to the mutual affections of two lovers, undiscovered to their friends.[1]

In practice a secretary was largely occupied with problems of security: the preservation of law and order within the country and the defence of the realm against plots hatched abroad or against possible foreign attack. Sir Francis Walsingham was particularly successful in this role of 'security officer' of the realm. He began his career as a protégé of Burghley. Between 1568 and 1570 he supplied Burghley with information about the movements of foreign spies in London, and in 1570, on the latter's suggestion, was nominated ambassador to France. In 1573 he was recalled, and in December of that year was appointed principal secretary. His work for the preservation of law and order within the realm can be illustrated by pointing to his role in securing the capture of Catholic priests who had entered the country to propagate their faith and who thus placed themselves at the mercy of the treason laws. It was largely due to the efficiency of the spy system which he organized in England that few priests were able to evade the government's grasp.[2]

As secretary Walsingham was also largely responsible for a task which takes us on to the second great role of Elizabethan government: the defence of the realm against foreign powers. Here his intelligence agents – scattered throughout Europe – had a significant part to play. They were not, of course, his only source of information about the machinations of foreign countries against England. Much news came from merchants, from friendly princes, and through ordinary diplomatic channels, but Walsingham's own spies were unquestionably very important. At one time he had in his pay 53 agents at foreign courts, besides eighteen other spies whose functions are more obscure. These men sent him a continuous stream of useful information; for example,

[1] R. Cecil, 'The State and Dignity of a secretary of state's place . . .', *Harleian Miscellany*, ii (1809), pp. 281–2.

[2] C. Read, *Mr. Secretary Walsingham and Queen Elizabeth*, i, 54ff, pp. 94–5, p. 263; ii, pp. 317–38.

details about the preparation of the Armada.[1] It was, of course, one thing to be informed about the dangers which threatened the country from abroad, quite another to be adequately prepared to defend the realm against such menaces. The practical responsibility for such defence lay with the army and navy.

The Elizabethan army has generally had a poor press from historians. A typical judgment is that of Sir Charles Oman. It is true, he admits, that, on occasion, Elizabeth put large numbers of troops in the field both for service abroad and for home defence at times of rebellion or threatened invasion: for example Leicester took nearly 10,000 men to the Netherlands in 1585 and at least 60,000 troops were assembled, in different places, to resist a possible Spanish landing in the Armada year, 1588. But, Oman, goes on, 'all these forces were very unsatisfactory gatherings of haphazard material, and ... organization was terribly deficient and military training usually contemptible'. This picture is undoubtedly true, and makes one wonder what would have happened if a sizeable force of veteran Spanish troops had ever managed to land in England. The poor state of the army was, however, bound to continue as long as it consisted of raw country levies officered and supplied by captains and merchants who exploited the men ruthlessly by means of an infinite variety of corrupt practices. Too much blame should not be laid at the door of the Queen and the Privy Council; they made serious efforts to improve the lot of the common soldier and generally did their best in a difficult situation. The real solution lay in a standing army under the close control of the Crown, but that was not a practicable solution at the time, largely for financial reasons.[2]

The army, though it fought campaigns abroad and in Ireland which the Queen certainly considered as largely defensive measures against Spain, was never put to the test of defending England against an actual invasion. This, of course, was not true of the navy, whose moment of greatest glory came in 1588. Elizabeth did not greatly increase the size of the fleet during her reign, but in quality it was unquestionably the finest in existence.

[1] C. Read, *Mr. Secretary Walsingham and Queen Elizabeth*, ii, pp. 369–70; iii, p. 285ff. *Dictionary of National Biography, sub* Walsingham, Sir Francis.

[2] C. Oman, *A History of the Art of War in the Sixteenth Century* (1937), 372–3. The best account of the Elizabethan army is by C. G. Cruickshank, *Elizabeth's Army* (2nd ed., Oxford, 1966).

This suggests that the administration behind it must have been at least relatively efficient, a supposition which is borne out by the facts. Naval organization had been revolutionized by Henry VIII in 1546, the date of the foundation of what later became known as the Navy Board. The most important officer was the Treasurer, who was in practice the senior executive official of the Board. There were three Treasurers during Elizabeth's reign. One of these, Fulke Grevill, who occupied the office for a few years at the end of the century, seems to have made little impact, but the other two were important figures. Benjamin Gonson, who had become Treasurer in 1549, retained the office until his death in 1577. He was certainly a competent public servant, but is overshadowed by his son-in-law and successor, John Hawkins, one of the most notable figures of Elizabethan administrative history. Hawkins, already famous as a commander at sea, held the Treasurership until 1595, and was thus in office during one of the most crucial periods in English naval history. He was the organizer of victories in the naval struggle against Spain, superintending the building, equipping and repairing of ships, the supply of adequate stores, and indeed all administrative details except those connected with ordnance and with the recruiting and victualling of the men. It was an immense task, but it did not prevent him finding time to make very important technical innovations. The finest Elizabethan men-of-war were built from his plans: from his term of office date the relatively low and long English fighting ships – the ships which proved so much more efficient than their relatively unwieldy Spanish opponents.[1]

The cost of naval and military operations was, of course, high and produced great difficulties for the government, especially in the Queen's last years. This consideration introduces the third main task of the central administration: that of raising enough money to ensure the government and defence of the realm. As already noted[2] the average annual revenue of the Crown rose from about £265,000 in the early years of the reign to approximately £490,000 during the last years of the century. During the

[1] M. Oppenheim, *A History of the Administration of the Royal Navy . . . 1509 to 1660* (1896), 85–6, 115, 126–7, 144–9, 184.

[2] On p. 8 above.

Elizabethan period three institutions played a part in the collection and administration of that money: the Court of Wards, the Duchy of Lancaster, and the Exchequer, the first two being of essentially minor importance as far as the size of their turnover was concerned. The net income of the Court of Wards (responsible for feudal revenues) averaged about £15,000 per annum during the reign, that of the Duchy of Lancaster (responsible for its own lands) between £10,000 and £12,000. All the rest of the royal revenue – the vast bulk of it – was thus administered by the Exchequer. This supremacy of the Exchequer, the traditional body for the control of the royal finances, had been restored only a few years before Elizabeth came to the throne. The development of the 'Chamber system' of finance from the later fifteenth century and the creation by Henry VIII and Thomas Cromwell of new institutions to administer the vast increase in the Crown's revenue brought about by the Reformation and the dissolution of the monasteries led to a situation in which by 1542 the royal finances were administered by six departments: the Exchequer, the Duchy of Lancaster, the Court of Wards and Liveries, the Court of General Surveyors, the Court of Augmentations, and the Court of First Fruits and Tenths. Within twelve years the last three institutions had lost their independent existence. The Court of General Surveyors (which dealt with the lands acquired by Henry VII and Wolsey) and the Court of Augmentations (responsible for lands acquired by the dissolution of the monasteries) were combined in 1547, and seven years later, together with the Court of First Fruits and Tenths (responsible for ecclesiastical revenue acquired at the time of the Reformation), were absorbed into the Exchequer.[1]

The history of the Elizabethan Exchequer has yet to be written, but one thing is certain; that history is intimately bound up with the ideas of the two men who served Elizabeth in the office of Lord Treasurer for all but the last five years of her reign. The first of these was Sir William Paulet, first Marquess of Winchester. Historians have yet to reveal the details of Winchester's work, a task in which they have been hampered both by the length of

[1] For these developments see W. C. Richardson, *Tudor Chamber Administration 1485–1547* (Baton Rouge, 1952), *passim*; G. R. Elton, *The Tudor Revolution in Government* (Cambridge, 1953), p. 20ff; B. P. Woolffe, 'The Management of English Royal Estates under the Yorkist Kings', *EHR*, lxxi (1956), 1ff.

his career (he was born in 1485 and held the Lord Treasurership from 1550 until his death in 1572) and by the illegibility of his handwriting. There is no doubt about his importance. He was one of the great administrators of Tudor England, the most important link between the ages of Cromwell and Burghley, and the man behind the restoration of Exchequer supremacy in 1554. This reform led to a transformation in the position of the Lord Treasurer, whose office had previously been largely an honorary one. Winchester was the first of the line of Lord Treasurers who were not only in practical terms ministers of finance and thus key figures in the whole administrative system, but also, during the sixteenth and seventeenth centuries, often chief ministers of the Crown as well.[1]

Granted his responsibility for the reforms of 1554, Winchester may be rated as a man of some imagination and vision. It is less easy to see Burghley in that light. As a financial administrator – indeed in his attitude to the central administration generally – Burghley was overwhelmingly conservative. Professor Read sums up his discussion of Burghley's work as Lord Treasurer by concluding that 'he accepted the existing system as it was [and] never attempted any fundamental reforms'.[2] Dr. Brian Outhwaite in his recent study of Elizabethan finance presents a similar picture, being particularly severe on Burghley's failure to make any significant effort to increase the real value of the Crown's ordinary revenue.[3] Examination of Burghley's work as Master of the Court of Wards leaves an exactly similar impression. As Master he was responsible for all those who succeeded under age to land held in chief of the Crown. At the beginning of his mastership he was selling over eighty per cent of such wardships for less than one and a half times the annual value of the wards' lands. In 1598, at the very end of his mastership, just under eighty per cent were being sold at the same rate. In other words, despite the Crown's increasingly pressing financial needs, he did little or

[1] For suggestive comments on Winchester see W. C. Richardson, *Tudor Chamber Administration*, pp. 433–4; W. C. Richardson, *History of the Court of Augmentations 1536–1554* (Baton Rouge, 1961), p. 454ff; G. R. Elton, *The Tudor Revolution in Government*, pp. 256–8.

[2] C. Read, *Lord Burghley and Queen Elizabeth* (1960), p. 84.

[3] R. B. Outhwaite, 'Studies in Elizabethan Government Finance: Royal borrowing and the sale of Crown lands, 1572–1603', (Nottingham University Ph.D. thesis, 1964). See especially Chapter 1.

nothing to raise the revenue from wardships. Just what could be done in this field was shown by Sir Robert Cecil. Immediately on becoming Master of the Wards in 1599 he raised the selling price of wardships to three or four times the annual value of the lands. As a result, in 1603, only five years after Burghley's death, revenue from the sale of wardships was over three times as great as it had been at the end of his mastership.[1] It is clear, indeed, that Burghley's abilities as an administrator lay in his diligence and in his economy, not in any breadth of vision. We noticed in an earlier chapter that Elizabeth's continuing solvency was one of the great achievements of her reign. Much of the credit for that solvency must go to Burghley as well as to the Queen; both realized the need to conserve the country's resources and both worked hard in practice to keep expenses down. Yet Burghley's stress on economy was a weakness as well as a strength. It narrowed his vision and was one factor in preventing him from attempting to achieve much needed increases in the Crown's ordinary revenue. As a result, Elizabeth, with the mounting expenses of her later years, had to ask for more and more parliamentary subsidies. The increasing difficulties which she experienced with Parliament at the end of the century were a direct result of this situation, though it was the Stuarts who really reaped the consequences after 1603.

The raising of enough money to ensure the protection and administration of the realm; the defence of the country against foreign powers; the preservation of law and order within England: these were the fundamental tasks of any sixteenth century government. Some way behind them, but still important, was the obligation to take a paternalistic interest in the welfare of the subject. This duty was reflected in much of the social and economic legislation of the reign; in the ever increasing administrative responsibilities which were heaped upon the J.P.s in such matters as the poor law; and in the watchful eye which the Privy Council kept upon a host of matters which affected subjects' well-being. It was also reflected in the work of many of the institutions of central government. The equitable jurisdiction of such bodies as the Councils in the Marches and in the North and, more notably, the Courts of Chancery and Requests, symbolized the Queen's obligation and desire to see that justice was done to all. Very

[1] J. Hurstfield, 'Lord Burghley as Master of the Court of Wards', *Transactions of the Royal Historical Society*, 4th series, xxxi (1949), 113.

clearly, that aim was not always realized, but the intention was there. As far as the upper reaches of society were concerned, the Court of Wards played an important part in the upbringing of young men and women who would later take their places among the most important of the Queen's subjects. During his long mastership Burghley revealed that he was very conscious of the responsibilities which this placed upon him.[1]

Discussion of the institutions of central government has so far revealed little about the men who staffed them, their backgrounds and the methods by which they were recruited and paid. Some knowledge of such matters is, however, essential for any full understanding of Elizabethan administration. The official 'civil service' – those men who received a salary or fees, or both, from the Crown in return for the administrative or judicial work which they performed – was very small, both relatively and absolutely, when compared with the vast army of public servants who run the country today. Officials of the central government probably numbered less than 1,000, some hundreds in London and some hundreds in the provinces.[2]

Let us look at the establishment of a single department, the Court of Wards, with less than a dozen on its London payroll, but over forty officers in the localities.[3] The officials in London were appointed by the Queen – no doubt after she had consulted the Master – but the representatives of the Court in the counties, the feodaries, were nominated directly by the Master. This was typical of arrangements in most departments of state. The Crown generally appointed the highest officials, and the administrative head or heads of the department had the patronage of the lesser offices. Officials of the Court of Wards usually came, as one might expect, from the gentry class – the feodaries from among the lesser gentry. They received salaries from the Queen and additional fees for their prescribed administrative duties, but these sources of

[1] J. Hurstfield, *The Queen's Wards* (1958), p. 241ff.

[2] Professor MacCaffrey makes some estimate of the number of government officials in 'Place and Patronage in Elizabethan Politics', *Elizabethan Government and Society* (eds. S. T. Bindoff, J. Hurstfield, C. H. Williams, 1961), pp. 106–8. See also F. Peck, *Desiderata Curiosa*, i (1732), book ii, 1ff.

[3] On the officials of the Court of Wards see H. E. Bell, *Introduction to the History and Records of the Court of Wards and Liveries* (Cambridge, 1953), pp. 16–45; J. Hurstfield, *The Queen's Wards*, pp. 221–40.

income were supplemented by the gratuities or tips which they obtained from suitors who wished to secure their goodwill in wardship transactions. Again this pattern can be found repeated in other administrative departments. Salaries, fees and gratuities were the three sources on which civil servants depended for their livelihood. Salaries tended to be small and fees to be fixed or limited but the amount obtained from gratuities was restricted only by the capacity and willingness of suitors to pay and the greed of the official concerned. Clearly unscrupulous officials who were important enough to be able to satisfy their clients' desires could obtain very large sums from this source.

To consider only established civil servants would, however, be to give an entirely false impression of the machinery of government. An important salaried official in a central department was usually surrounded by private secretaries and clerks, whom he appointed personally and who were responsible to him alone. They often performed important duties – many officials could not have done their work without such personal assistants – yet they were sometimes completely dependent for their remuneration on the gratuities of clients who had business with their masters and hoped to ease their path by judicious tips to underlings. Such a system, which gave these personal assistants influence without official responsibility for their actions was clearly a dangerous one, yet it pervaded the entire Elizabethan administrative machinery – to take an extreme case each of the six Clerks of Chancery might employ upwards of forty subordinates[1] – and it is difficult to see what solution could have been found. The government simply did not have the resources to pay for the adequate staffing of the departments of state on an official basis.

Under this system many personal assistants must have made at least tolerably satisfactory livings, but few, if any, had the opportunities which were open to Burghley's secretary, Michael Hickes, who became a wealthy man and lent money to peers of the realm during the 1590s. Burghley's secretaries certainly played significant roles in the administration of the country.[2] During the last

[1] W. J. Jones, 'The Elizabethan Chancery: some legal and other apsects', (London University Ph.D. thesis, 1958), p. 104.

[2] For a detailed discussion of the evidence see A. G. R. Smith, 'Sir Michael Hickes and the secretariat of the Cecils, circa 1580–1612', (London University Ph.D. thesis, 1962), chapters 3, 5 and 9.

twenty years or so of his life, when there is relatively plentiful information about his secretariat, he had, at any one time, either three or four secretaries, of whom Hickes and Henry Maynard were much the most important. Maynard specialized in foreign affairs, dealing with the business of countries which ranged from Scotland to Germany and also with naval and military problems. His concern with these 'matters of state' reflected the fact that Burghley, the principal minister of the Crown, was intimately concerned with the whole field of the country's foreign relations. Maynard sometimes complained of being over-burdened with work and it is clear that a vast volume of business passed through his hands. His colleague Michael Hickes specialized in another field. He was patronage secretary, controlling to a great extent that access to Burghley which could be so important in furthering suitors' ambitions. The work of Hickes and Maynard and their colleagues in Burghley's secretariat can be paralleled by the duties performed by the private secretaries of other Elizabethan ministers, such as Sir Francis Walsingham and Sir Robert Cecil. In 1603 the latter had four personal assistants, who helped him with his work as secretary of state and Master of the Wards, while Walsingham, during his occupancy of the secretaryship between 1573 and 1590, had a multitude of confidential clerks.

The important roles which the personal assistants of ministers and high officials played in the government of the country indicates the need for great caution before applying a word like 'bureaucratic' to the administrative system, and leaving it at that. The very essence of the private offices of ministers and officials was that they were not bureaucratic machines with settled staffs and procedures. The clerks and secretaries who served in them were appointed and dismissed entirely at the will of their masters, who organized the work of their private offices as they thought best. These private clerks, in other words, though they did government business, were essentially members of their masters' households. The Elizabethan administrative system, in fact, was a mixture of 'bureaucratic' and 'household' elements, of established officials working through permanent institutions with fixed procedures, and of private secretaries and assistants working in the offices of ministers and other leading administrators in whatever ways their masters thought best at any given moment.

CHAPTER FIVE

The Patronage System

THOUGH many of the institutions of the central government were thus designed to preserve law and order throughout the realm, it is a commonplace that the coercive power of Elizabeth's government was limited. With no large paid bureaucracy in the localities and no standing army the Queen had to rely largely on political persuasion to secure and keep internal peace and stability. To this end she depended, not only on successful exploitation of the mystique of monarchy, but also on her capacity to reward her more prominent subjects by sharing out the offices, prestige and wealth at her disposal, in other words on the distribution of patronage.

Any sixteenth-century government lived under a threat of violent resistance to its will. Parliament met only occasionally and for short periods at a time and disappointed politicians and noblemen, unable to resort to protracted parliamentary intrigue, might be tempted to indulge in conspiracy and treason, as in the Northern Rebellion of 1569 and the Essex Revolt of 1601, each of them a frontal challenge to the Elizabethan political system. In these circumstances the Queen and her ministers had to exercise constant vigilance in order to anticipate and try to prevent plots against the state. In addition, however, Elizabeth endeavoured, by as fair a distribution of the Crown's favours as possible, to link the material interests of the politically conscious members of the Elizabethan nation with the fate of the government. Her use of patronage was aimed in the words of a recent authority, 'not at the adherence of a party or faction but at the goodwill and confidence of a whole class.'[1]

First among the various kinds of benefits at the Queen's disposal were grants of honours, notably peerages and knighthoods. Henry VII was sparing in the creation of peers, but Henry VIII

[1] W. T. MacCaffrey, 'Place and Patronage in Elizabethan Politics', *Elizabethan Government and Society*, p. 98.

in his later years raised up many new noble houses and this proliferation continued during the reign of Edward VI. Between 1509 and 1553 a total of forty-seven peerages were created or restored. Elizabeth returned to the frugal policy of her grandfather. She created or recognized only eighteen peerages, of which eight were either restorations of former titles or admissions of inheritance through the female line. In fact, as fourteen noble families became extinct during the reign and as six other titles lapsed due to attainders, there were fewer peers in 1603 than there had been in 1558, fifty-five as compared with fifty-seven.[1]

The Queen was also sparing in the creation of knights. At her accession there were perhaps 600 in the country, but by 1580 the number had fallen to about 300. It did increase during the last two decades of the reign, but this was largely because of creations by military commanders during the wars of the period. The Earl of Essex was especially generous in his distribution of knighthoods. He dubbed twenty-one men during the French expedition of 1591, joined with Lord Howard of Effingham to create sixty-eight on the Cadiz expedition of 1596, and made as many as eighty-one during his disastrous Irish campaign of 1599. Some of these Essex knights were of such lowly origin and small fortune as to arouse general derision. This attitude was reflected in the popular rhyme,

> A knight of Cales [Cadiz],
> And a gentleman of Wales,
> And a laird of the North-Countree,
> A yeoman of Kent
> With his yearly rent
> Will buy them out all three.

As a result of these bursts of new creations the total number of knights probably increased by about 250 during the last twenty years of the reign, making a total of around 550 in 1603, of whom over a quarter had been created by Essex.[2]

Elizabeth's attitude to the distribution of honours clearly reflected her social conservatism. She was so sparing in her creation of peers that each grant of a title of nobility was a great occasion. The dignity of the peerage remained very high throughout the reign. The position as regards knighthoods is more com-

[1] L. Stone, *The Crisis of the Aristocracy 1558–1641*, pp. 97–9.
[2] *Ibid.*, pp. 71–3.

plicated. Here, the Queen's personal parsimony in creations coupled with the lavish grants of the Earl of Essex produced, by the end of the reign, a situation in which middle-aged members of the substantial gentry who had not engaged in the military expeditions of the 1590s had to make do with the title of esquire, while many younger, poorer, and often very much less worthy men who had gone adventuring in the wars had achieved the dignity of knighthood. This was a state of affairs which infuriated the Queen. She had specifically ordered Essex to be sparing in his creations during the Irish Expedition of 1599, and when he ignored her commands she actually thought of depriving the new knights of their precedence in public ceremonies, an extreme step from which she was deterred only by the arguments of Cecil. It would be going much too far to say that the honour of knighthood had fallen into disrepute by the end of Elizabeth's reign. After all, as already noted, there were probably fewer knights in 1603 than in 1558. Nevertheless, the very uneven distribution of the honour during the closing years of the century certainly caused ill feeling among the wealthier gentry.[1]

A second source of patronage lay in the great array of offices at the Crown's disposal: posts in the Church, Court, judiciary, central and regional administrations, military and naval services, and in the royal land administration. These varied in importance from the greatest offices of state such as the Lord Chancellorship, and Lord Treasurership to numerous posts connected with the management of the royal lands, such as stewardships of manors and keeperships of parks and houses.[2] Professor MacCaffrey has calculated that, neglecting ecclesiastical benefices, the Crown 'was able to dispose of about 1,200 places worth a gentleman's having', and that, allowing for a certain amount of pluralism there must have been 'at least 1,000 gentlemen – placemen at any given moment in Elizabeth's reign'. He has also estimated that the number of men in England during this period who at any one time took a direct and intelligent interest in politics was not more than 2,500.[3] If these figures are correct[4] forty per cent of the

[1] *Ibid.*, pp. 73–4.

[2] W. T. MacCaffrey, 'Place and Patronage in Elizabethan Politics', *Elizabethan Government and Society*, pp. 106–8, 123–4.

[3] *Ibid.*, pp. 99, 108.

[4] They have recently been criticized by Professor Stone, *The Crisis of the Aristocracy 1558–1641*, 466–7.

politically conscious class in Elizabethan England held profitable offices under the Crown.

A third important source of benefit for fortunate subjects was the Queen's lands. These could be leased to favoured parties on specially advantageous terms, and those who secured such grants included minor officials of the Queen's household as well as great court favourites.[1] Another form of royal bounty was pensions or annuities. About 350 people were receiving annuities in 1573. Some of these were retired servants of the Crown but a large proportion were active courtiers with other sources of income. Great noblemen like Buckhurst and Leicester headed the list. The latter had £1,000 a year out of the customs, but a pension of this size was quite exceptional. Few annuities in fact rose above £20 or £30 a year.[2]

A fifth form of patronage consisted of grants of export licences, customs farms and monopolies, all of which stemmed from the Crown's prerogative right to regulate the economic life of the country. Export licences, which exempted recipients from statutes forbidding certain kinds of exports, and farms of the royal customs could be very valuable and were often granted to court favourites. Leicester and later Essex had the farm of sweet wines and Hatton that of French wines. Monopolies, the sole right to make or distribute particular products, were originally allowed in order to reward inventions and to encourage new arts and manufactures. During the 1580s and 1590s, however, numerous monopolies were granted which affected already established industries, making large profits for the grantees but raising prices for the consumer. This situation produced rumblings of discontent in the Parliament of 1597, when the Queen promised redress. Nothing, however, was done. Indeed, the situation got worse. In the four years after 1597 at least thirty new patents were issued, including grants for currants, iron, bottles, vinegar, steel, brushes, pots, salt, lead and oil. The result was the great monopolies crisis in the Parliament of 1601, which forced the Queen to take action to restrict abuses. Clearly, Elizabeth's indiscriminate granting of patents in the 1580s and 1590s was foolish in political terms and it is reasonable to conclude that she handled the distribution

[1] *Ibid.*, p. 405; W. T. MacCaffrey, 'Place and Patronage in Elizabethan Politics', *Elizabethan Government and Society*, pp. 114, 121.
[2] *Ibid.*, 114–5.

of this section of her store of patronage with no great skill. However, the difficulty of her position should be recognized. Monopolies became increasingly numerous and really obnoxious to the subject only during the last fifteen years of the reign. These of course were also years of war with Spain, years when the Queen's increasing financial liabilities abroad made it more and more difficult for her to reward her servants at home. One way in which she could do so without parting with money was by granting patents of monopoly. It is sufficient to note, in this connection, that a very large number of monopolists were courtiers of middle rank.[1]

Titles of honour; offices; leases of Crown lands; pensions; monopolies and allied grants: this is not an exhaustive list of favours in the Crown's gift, but it does include the main categories. The great majority of those who benefited from this stock of patronage came, as we have seen, from the 2,500 or so persons who formed, at any one moment, the politically conscious part of the Elizabethan nation. These can be divided into two groups. The first and by far the largest group comprised those members of the gentry class who had no claims to direct contact with the sovereign together with a number of aspiring lawyers, dons and other townsmen. Many members of this group were relentless in their search for favours. They either thronged the Court, soliciting suits in person, or else pursued their petitions by letter from a distance. Between such suitors and the Queen, the nominal source of all benefits, stood the second group, those great officials and favourites who not only had direct access to the sovereign and could thus solicit clients' suits, but also themselves, by reason of their offices, disposed of a large portion of the royal store of patronage. Interposed between the two groups were the secretaries and personal assistants of the great officers of state and leading courtiers. These were the 'contact men' of the patronage system, often putting members of the first group in touch with the great men of the second and receiving in return a flood of tips or gratuities from grateful suitors. One of these personal assistants was Michael Hickes, already mentioned as secretary to Burghley, a post he occupied from 1580 until 1598. Because of his master's enormous influence in the distribution of patronage

---

[1] *Ibid.*, pp. 120–21; W. H. Price, *English Patents of Monopoly* (Boston, Massachusetts, 1906), 8–21.

Hickes was courted by great numbers of clients, all of them
anxious to obtain his word in Burghley's ear in favour of their
suits and the majority of them ready to pay for his services.
Hickes made his own attitude to gratuities perfectly clear in a
letter to his friend Roger Manners, when he assured him of his
'honest, true affection' and remarked that he was able to give
proof of this now and again 'in these petty kind of offices ...
which I know are as welcome and acceptable to you as twenty
fair angels[1] laid in the hands of us poor bribers here in Court'.[2]
Suitors often offered Hickes large sums to secure his favour – £100
and 100 angels are examples – but a gratuity did not have to be
money: he was also promised bucks, geldings, and on one occasion
even a 'Welsh nag' worth £5.[3] This practice of giving and receiving tips, which, as already pointed out, pervaded the entire
Elizabethan administrative system, was generally accepted by
everybody from the highest officers of state downwards. Gratuities
were essential to secure an adequate standard of living for government servants.

Ministers and courtiers were clearly both recipients and dispensers of patronage. They were recipients because they held
their offices or obtained their influence from the Crown; they
were dispensers because they used their positions to advance the
suits of others. It follows that the more influential an official
was, the greater the number of his clients. Burghley was overwhelmed with suitors. A contemporary tells us that he received
between sixty and one hundred letters a day from clients.[4]
Other leading figures, men like Walsingham and Hatton, had
their own circles of suitors, but, before the 1590s, only Leicester
rivalled Burghley in the number and eminence of his clients.
Leicester did not hold any of those great offices of state, such as
the Chancellorship of the Duchy of Lancaster, which in themselves brought their holders considerable patronage. His great
influence simply derived from his position as the Queen's favourite. From the very beginning of the reign he seems to have played
an important backstage role in the making of appointments and

1 An angel was an Elizabethan coin worth 10s.

2 British Museum Lansdowne Manuscript 107, f162r.

3 British Museum Lansdowne Manuscripts, 66, f161r; 86, f77r; 77, f127r;
108, f96r; 83, f114r.

4 F. Peck, *Desiderata Curiosa*, i, book i, p. 19.

in the conferring of favours, and his power, when it became known, soon brought him substantial monetary benefits. Eleven corporations, nine bishops, two deans and chapters and both universities granted him annuities or sinecure offices which carried fees.[1] In return they no doubt secured his assistance in their suits to the Queen.

The workings of the patronage system thus produced a host of middlemen of all ranks who stood, hands outstretched for gratuities, between suitors and their goals. The importance of such intermediaries can be illustrated statistically by referring to their role in wardship business. The Queen received about £650,000 in all from wardship during her reign, but it has been estimated that the purchasers of wardships and the lessees of wards' lands paid perhaps four times as much, about £2,600,000. The difference between the sum which the Queen obtained and that which the purchasers and lessees paid represented money handed over to middlemen of one kind or another, mostly courtiers and civil servants.[2]

Clearly, then, all sections of the Elizabethan political community, from courtiers and ministers of state to lesser members of the the gentry class, benefited from the workings of the patronage system. This reflected the Queen's determination to spread the favours at her disposal among as wide a circle of her deserving subjects as possible. She did this by refusing to limit her confidence to a single minister or favourite. She thus kept open a number of channels through which the Crown's patronage could be obtained. This policy had a profound effect on the structure of politics. It led to the formation of factions around each of the leading figures of the period and to struggles among the faction leaders, each of whom tried to gain greater influence with the Queen and thus a more important voice in the distribution of patronage.

This system of government by faction worked reasonably well throughout the greater part of the reign and only broke down in the 1590s. There were two reasons why it worked well for so long. Firstly, there was the fact that nobody, until late in the reign, challenged its basic premise: namely that the Queen's confidence

[1] W. T. MacCaffrey, 'Elizabethan Politics: the First Decade, 1558–1568', *Past and Present*, April 1963, p. 34; L. Stone, *The Crisis of the Aristocracy 1558–1641*, p. 446.

[2] J. Hurstfield, *The Queen's Wards*, pp. 345–7.

and the royal patronage should not be monopolized by a single person. There was thus a fundamental harmony of outlook between the Queen and the leading statesmen of the first half of the reign, none of whom attempted to gain complete control of the patronage machine. The second reason why the system worked well is to be found in the position which Burghley came to occupy within it. As has just been stressed, he was not the only person through whom royal favours flowed, but no one else enjoyed the Queen's confidence to the extent that he did. Other courtiers and ministers could always initiate and advance suits but more and more as the years passed Burghley's approval was often decisive. In part his great influence reflected the fact that from 1561 he was Master of the Court of Wards and from 1572 Lord Treasurer as well. Each of these offices gave him direct or indirect control of a large number of government appointments and favours. But he was also on friendly terms with almost all members of the peerage throughout the reign. Great noblemen like the Earls of Huntingdon, Bedford, Shrewsbury and Warwick benefited from his favour. These men had independent influence with the Queen, but they often found that benefits which they obtained for themselves or their clients 'could only be profitable if Burghley approved the particular terms and conditions which made the grant valuable'.[1] Burghley used his great authority and experience with moderation, never attempting to obtain a complete monopoly of the Queen's confidence. Perhaps he realized that if he had done so he would have forfeited the very basis of his influence, the Queen's trust. At any rate, whatever his motives, he acted as much more than a faction leader. For most of the reign the Queen and he together, by judicious management of the patronage machinery, secured the loyalty of the great majority of the politically conscious members of the Elizabethan community. In 1598, however, he died.

The years after his death saw the climax of the conflict between his son Sir Robert Cecil and the Earl of Essex, which had begun in the early 1590s but which reached its tragic culmination only with the Essex Revolt of 1601. The Essex–Cecil struggle was one of two closely interrelated and very important political developments of the 1590s which were symptoms of the breakdown of the

[1] W. T. MacCaffrey, 'Place and Patronage in Elizabethan Politics', *Elizabethan Government and Society*, pp. 109–10.

classic Elizabethan system. The other was the growth of corruption in the public service, a phenomenon to which our attention was first drawn nearly twenty years ago.[1] There is evidence that, during the last decade of the reign, the generally accepted practice of giving and receiving gratuities degenerated into a system which was little better than outright bribery, with suitors feverishly competing for places and favours. There were probably two main reasons for this decline in political morality. One was the war with Spain. Its enormous cost caused the Queen, as the 1590s progressed, to reduce more and more her gifts and favours to courtiers and suitors. 'What little gain there is gotten in this time', wailed one in 1594, and in 1600 Elizabeth herself apologized because war expenses had forced her to 'restrain her bountiful hand from rewarding her servants.'[2] In these circumstances it was natural that there should be increased competition for such benefits as remained, with suitors offering and courtiers accepting larger and larger gratuities, which soon became indistinguishable from bribes.

The other important reason for the decline in official probity was the emergence of a new generation of politicians of whom the most important were the Earl of Essex and Sir Robert Cecil. In the 1590s Cecil, then undergoing his political apprenticeship, resorted to practices which did him little credit. He seems to have worked hand in glove during these years with Michael Hickes, who was his close personal friend as well as his father's secretary. In 1594–95, for example, Cecil and Hickes took part in a devious and disreputable plot to secure the appointment of the notoriously corrupt Toby Matthew to the bishopric of Durham. They finally obtained the see for him and almost certainly got a very substantial gratuity in return. Cecil's main fear during these negotiations seems to have been that the Queen would get to know of his scheming behind the scenes. He used his access to her at that time, he informed Hickes, in such a way that she could not suspect that he 'looked to anything but [her] service', a tacit admission that he was putting his own interests first![3] It is

---

[1] By J. E. Neale in 'The Elizabethan Political Scene', *Essays in Elizabethan History*, pp. 59–84.

[2] L. Stone, *The Crisis of the Aristocracy 1558–1641*, pp. 488–9.

[3] A. G. R. Smith, 'Sir Michael Hickes and the secretariat of the Cecils, circa 1580–1612', (London University Ph.D. thesis, 1962), pp. 173–8.

difficult to imagine Burghley resorting to such machinations in the high Elizabethan period.

Cecil's intrigues in the Toby Matthew case reflected the fact that, in the 1590s, each office in Church and state became a prize to be fought over by the rival factions of himself and Essex. The main reason for this lay in Essex's ambitions. The young earl, he was only twenty-eight in 1595, was a man of brilliance and charm who had a fatal flaw in his political make-up. He refused to accept the basis of the Elizabethan system: the axiom that the Queen's confidence and with it the distribution of patronage should not be limited to a single man. Essex wanted everything for himself and his followers and planned to become the sole source through whom the Crown's bounty flowed. If he had succeeded in achieving his ambition and placing his clients in all the key posts at Court and in the administration he would have become the real ruler of the country with the ageing Queen reduced, in effect, to a cipher. Elizabeth was as determined to resist the earl's inordinate ambitions as she was anxious not to humiliate him. She probably hoped for the development in due course of the kind of situation which had prevailed in the 1570s and 1580s when Leicester and Burghley, then the most powerful men in the state, provided the two main channels for the distribution of patronage. If that was indeed the Queen's idea – a repetition of the former balance between noble favourite and trusted administrator, with Essex filling the role of Leicester and Robert Cecil that of Burghley – her hopes were doomed. Essex had none of Leicester's essential moderation. His refusal to live and let live and his desire to dominate completely made him impervious to reason and, in the end, a major threat to the state.

Essex's efforts to build up his party and his rivalry with Cecil can be examined at several levels: in the country at large; in Parliament; in the Court and administration. In the country his influence was particularly strong in Wales and the Marches where in the 1580s and 1590s he built up a strong following. By 1601 many of his supporters there held important offices. For example, among the deputy lieutenants, Sir Gelly Meyrick and Roger Vaughan in Radnorshire, Francis Meyrick in Pembrokeshire, Sir Robert Salusbury and Sir Richard Trevor in Denbighshire, Sir Herbert Croft in Herefordshire, and Sir Henry Bromley in Worcestershire, were all friends of his. Sir Robert Cecil did not have a Welsh party of comparable strength, but he was able to build up a powerful position in northern England. There the Essex–Cecil struggle centred in attempts to gain control of the Council of the North, a contest which went on throughout the 1590s. Essex seems to have held the initial advantage, but Cecil triumphed in 1599 when he was able to secure the appointment of his brother, the second Lord Burghley, as Lord President.[1]

The rivalry of the two faction leaders was also reflected in the attention which they paid to parliamentary patronage. In 1597 in particular both Essex and Cecil conducted extensive election campaigns. Essex, then at the very pinnacle of his career, fresh from his dazzling triumph of 1596 at Cadiz, secured the election of eight of his servants to the Commons and also nominated a number of friends and relatives. These men, together with other followers and Essex knights who found their own seats, gave him a party in the Commons which may have numbered about thirty. Twelve of these M.P.s took part in the Essex Rebellion. Cecil was also able to secure a powerful following in this Parliament. His office of Chancellor of the Duchy of Lancaster gave him considerable facilities for placing his clients in the Lower House, but this alone did not satisfy him and he had recourse to the novel device of asking influential friends who were also borough patrons to transfer nominations which they controlled to himself: to give just one example, he received a seat at New Romney from his brother-in-law Lord Cobham.[2]

The influence which the two faction leaders built up in the country and in Parliament during the 1590s reflected the seriousness of the crucial struggle for power which was taking place at the centre of government: in the Court and administration. Here Cecil won decisively. The Queen, well aware of the limitless nature of Essex's ambitions, refused him high political office and his followers high political and court office. Essex was made Master of the Horse in 1587 and obtained the posts of Earl Marshal and Master of the Ordnance – neither of which conferred great patronage on the holder – in 1597. Cecil, in contrast, became principal secretary in 1596 and was appointed Chancellor

[1] P. Williams, *The Council in the Marches of Wales under Elizabeth I*, pp. 281–9; R. R. Reid, 'The North Parts under the Tudors', *Tudor Studies Presented to A. F. Pollard*, ed. R. W. Seton-Watson (1924), pp. 224–9.

[2] Neale, *Commons*, pp. 239–43.

of the Duchy of Lancaster in 1597. These two great offices of state carried immense political power and patronage and their bestowal was a clear indication of where the Queen's real confidence lay. She showed this even more plainly when, after Burghley's death, Essex strove desperately to obtain for himself the Mastership of the Wards with its vast attendant patronage. She refused him the prize and, after he had set out on his Irish adventure, conferred it on Cecil.[1]

Essex was conspicuously unsuccessful, too, in his attempts to secure high office for his friends and followers. On Walsingham's death in 1590 he tried to get William Davison restored to the secretaryship, from which he had been removed in 1587 for his part in the execution of Mary Queen of Scots. The Queen refused flatly and left the office vacant until 1596 when, as we have seen, Cecil was appointed. In 1593, when the post of Attorney-General was about to fall vacant, Essex started a violent campaign to secure it for his friend Francis Bacon, and when he finally saw that his efforts were in vain endeavoured to get Bacon the lesser office of Solicitor-General. Even that suit fell through, however. The Attorneyship went to a Cecilian, Sir Edward Coke, and the Solicitorship to an able lawyer, Serjeant Fleming. Essex believed, quite rightly, that these rebuffs reflected upon himself at least as much as upon Bacon. 'You fare ill', he told the latter, 'because you have chosen me for your mean and dependence', and with that generosity of spirit which was such an attractive aspect of his character insisted on compensating Bacon with a present of land – a gift which he could ill afford. In 1596 he tried to get the office of Lord Chamberlain for his friend Sir Robert Sidney and, when that attempt failed, engaged, in the following year, in a vain bid to obtain for him the Lord Wardenship of the Cinque ports. The two offices went in the end to the Lords Cobham, father and son, both of whom, significantly enough, were firmly attached to the Cecilian party. Essex was determined, however, to do something for Sidney. Early in 1598 he tried to get him a peerage and when Elizabeth refused announced that he was standing on Sidney's behalf against all-comers for the vacant office of Vicechamberlain. The Queen, however, left that post unfilled.[2]

[1] For the significance of the struggle over the Mastership of the Wards see J. Hurstfield, *The Queen's Wards*, chapter 14.

[2] J. E. Neale, *Queen Elizabeth*, pp. 330, 333–7, 347; *Commons*, pp, 214–5.

Essex put all his reputation at pledge in these suits. 'The Attorneyship for Francis [Bacon] is that I must have', he told Robert Cecil in 1594, 'and in that I will spend all my power, might, authority, and amity, and with tooth and nail defend and procure the same for him against whomsoever.' In such circumstances the Queen's refusals brought humiliation and led him to wild and irresponsible actions. He demanded that courtiers and officials should openly support him in his contest with Cecil and would allow no neutrality. 'My lord of Essex . . . has forced me to declare myself either his only, or friend to Mr. Secretary [Cecil]', wrote Lord Grey indignantly in 1598.[1] Many men faced with such a choice preferred the Cecilian side and the effect of Essex's dictum, 'He who is not with me is against me', was virtually to reduce the factions to two by 1601: his own and Cecil's.

This was the background of the Essex Revolt of February 1601. The Earl having tried to recoup his domestic failures by the Irish adventure of 1599 returned to England with his reputation and credit ruined. He was deeply in debt and in 1600 the Queen refused to renew his farm of the customs on sweet wines, the mainstay of his estate. This was a clear indication to the world that he would no longer be able to reward adequately the swarm of clients and suitors who thronged about him, and formed the basis of his power. His own solvency and his whole position as a faction leader were at stake. He gambled on rebellion; he lost; he was executed. But his failure, no less than if he had succeeded, spelled the end of the classic Elizabethan political and patronage systems which depended for their successful working on no one man obtaining a monopoly of power. Essex's attitude in the 1590s had reduced the factions to two. His fall left only that of Robert Cecil.

> Little Cecil trips up and down,
> He rules both Court and Crown,[2]

wrote a lampoonist after Essex's execution. His words were truer than he may have realized. Between 1601 and 1603 Cecil was, in effect, supreme.

[1] W. B. Devereux, *Lives and Letters of the Devereux, Earls of Essex*, i (1853), p. 285; Neale, *Commons*, p. 233.

[2] Cited J. E. Neale, *Queen Elizabeth*, p. 378.

CHAPTER SIX

Government Social and Economic Policy

DURING the sixteenth century there was a great increase in government intervention in the social and economic life of the country, as is shown by the flood of statutes and proclamations which dealt with economic problems. Perhaps the best way of discovering the motives which lay behind these economic measures is to recall the general aims of Elizabeth's government and to examine the economic and social legislation of the reign in the light of these aims.[1]

The main objectives of Elizabeth and her ministers were, it will be remembered, to preserve order within the country, to defend the realm against foreign powers, to raise enough money to ensure that England was adequately protected and administered, and finally, and some way behind the other aims, to take a paternalistic interest in the welfare of the people. In addition to these general considerations the economic and social policies of the government were influenced by the particular situation which faced it after 1558. Here the great economic fact was the depression which followed the collapse, in the early 1550s, of the boom associated with the growth of the cloth trade with the Netherlands during the early and middle years of the century.

The preservation of order within England was always a prime consideration in Elizabeth's policies. With no police force and no standing army a comparatively small disturbance could rapidly assume alarming proportions. In this connection legislation dealing with vagrancy and unemployment is significant. The harsh treatment meted out to vagabonds – and this theme will claim attention in more detail later on – reflected the government's determination to keep vagrancy under control and to ensure that it did not become a threat to public order.

[1] The best general account of the economic policies of Tudor governments is P. Ramsey, *Tudor Economic Problems*, (1963), pp. 146–79, to which this chapter is heavily indebted.

The preservation of the security of the realm in face of the threat of war and invasion was another fundamental duty of the government and its economic measures were often determined by military considerations. The active encouragement which it gave to the new mining and metallurgical enterprises of the reign, reflected in the incorporation of the Mines Royal Company and the Mineral and Battery Company in 1568, was designed largely to make the country independent of foreign ordnance.[1] Efforts made to improve seamanship had the specific objective of increasing the number of trained men at the disposal of the navy in the event of attempted foreign invasion. The notorious act of 1563,[2] appointing Wednesdays as compulsory days for eating fish in addition to Fridays and Saturdays, was designed to lead to a great increase in the size of the fishing fleet and consequently in the number of trained seamen. 'Cecil's fast', as it was known, was, in fact, primarily intended to strengthen the country's war potential and only incidentally meant to modify its dietary habits.

The third main aim of the government, the raising of enough money to ensure the administration and defence of the realm, is reflected in the pronounced fiscal element in many of its economic measures. Patents of monopoly, it will be recalled, were designed in theory to give protection to new or struggling industries or industries of national importance. By the end of the reign, however, they had become a means to supplement the inadequate salaries of officials or simply to gratify favourites. The Queen admitted as much in 1601 when she stated that many monopolies had been granted 'to particular persons, which have sustained losses and hindrances by service at sea and land, or such as have been her Majesty's ancient domestical servitors, or for some other like considerations'.[3] Indeed towards the end of the reign the whole system of economic controls became less and less a means of serving the national advantage and more and more a system for bringing fiscal profit to a Crown whose needs were constantly growing as a result of war and continuing inflation.[4]

[1] L. Stone, 'State control in sixteenth-century England', *EcHR*, xvii, (1947), p. 112.
[2] 5 Eliz., c.5.
[3] Cited, W. H. Price, *English Patents of Monopoly*, p. 157.
[4] On this point see, e.g. L. Stone, *The Crisis of the Aristocracy 1558–1641*, p. 424ff.

It is true, however, that Elizabeth's government did consider itself as having a duty to advance and protect the welfare of its subjects. That duty might be overshadowed by the fundamental necessities of preserving order, ensuring adequate national defence, and raising revenue, but it was an obligation which the government never entirely forgot. The government's paternalistic concern for the people can be seen, for example, in acts directed against forestallers and regrators.[1] Forestallers were men who cornered supplies of scarce goods, including foodstuffs, before they reached the market and then exploited their temporary local monopoly to force prices up. Regrators were those who bought and sold goods within a market and raised prices by taking a profit for services which were of no apparent use to anyone – except of course to themselves. Government measures against such men certainly reflected a desire to protect the consumer. The government also took action to prevent the export of foodstuffs in times of scarcity. To take just one instance, in 1597 the Privy Council regulated the quantities of herrings which might be exported from Yarmouth.[2] Again, the development of the poor law in the Elizabethan period shows an increasing concern for the genuinely unfortunate as well as a continuing determination to punish sturdy rogues and vagabonds.

Although the economic legislation of the period was shaped largely by the general non-economic aims of the government it was influenced too by the economic situation which confronted the country in 1558. The third quarter of the century was a period of slumps and depressions following the collapse in 1552 of the boom in cloth exports, and it has been suggested by Professor F. J. Fisher[3] that the economic policy of Elizabeth's government should be seen essentially as a reaction to the problems posed by this depression:

the depressions of the third quarter of the sixteenth century were a not unimportant episode in English economic history for they saw an erratic attempt to mould the economic system according to something like a pattern: . . . economic nationalism, the opening of distant markets and the organization of those already in existence, the encouragement

---

[1] 1 Eliz., c. 18; 5 Eliz., c 12; 15 Eliz., c. 25.

[2] R. H. Tawney and E. Power, *Tudor Economic Documents*, i (1924), pp. 166–7.

[3] 'Commercial trends and policy in sixteenth century England', *EcHR*, x (1939–40), pp. 95–117.

of new industries and the control of production in the old, the regulation of the whole pace of economic change and the public provision for the unemployed.[1]

Fisher's thesis has been subjected to severe criticism[2] and it is likely that he underestimates the extent of continuity between government policy in the early and later parts of the century and overestimates the extent of the Elizabethan depression. These criticisms, though they must be taken into account, do not, however, destroy the value of his arguments. For example his linking of the Elizabethan depression with the genesis of the statute of artificers and the development of the poor law[3] seems both valid and important.

The Elizabethan legislation on the poor was one of the two most elaborate attempts at social engineering in the Tudor period – the statute of artificers was the other – and detailed considera-tion of its development and effects reveals much about the ideas which motivated the Queen's government. From the early sixteenth century onwards there was a great upsurge of interest in England in the problems of poverty and vagrancy. This growth of interest was caused, almost certainly, by an increase in the number of vagrants: contemporary records are full of complaints about the great and growing number of vagabonds. Some of these accounts doubtless exaggerate but it seems certain that the number of vagrants and of the poor generally did grow. This increase was caused by economic and social changes which made themselves felt from the early sixteenth century onwards; notably population growth combined with a rapid inflation in which prices rose more quickly than wages, and accompanied by the upheavals which attended the periods of boom and depression in the cloth industry. Vagrants could be a serious threat to public order and it was certain that the Tudor authorities, with their horror of anything that might disturb the peace, would take measures to deal with them. The governments of the early Tudor period were certainly very alive to the problem and the Elizabethan legislation on the poor was partly a development of early sixteenth

[1] *Ibid.*, p. 116.

[2] Notably by L. Stone, 'State control in sixteenth century England', *EcHR*, xvii (1947), pp. 103–20.

[3] F. J. Fisher, 'Commercial trends and policy in sixteenth century England' *EcHR*, x (1939–40), pp. 113, 116.

century acts of parliament and partly an elaboration of measures
which some towns had introduced in advance of the national
system.[1]

The first Tudor act[2] dealing with the problem was one of 1495
which provided that vagabonds were to be put in the stocks for
three days on bread and water. This rigorous measure reflected
long established precedent. Medieval legislation against vagabondage, particularly that of the reign of Richard II, had been
notable for its savagery. The whole question of poverty and vagabondage was, however, taken up with some freshness in the reign
of Henry VIII. England's alliance with France in 1528 precipi-
tated an economic crisis since it paralysed the cloth trade with
the Netherlands, threw thousands out of work and thus led to a
sharp increase in the number of vagrants and of the poor. The
statute of 1531[3] stemmed from this situation. Its significance was
that it made the first real attempt to separate the worthy poor
from the vagabonds. It provided that vagrants and unruly
persons were to be whipped and returned to their homes, while
the impotent poor were to be licensed to beg in their own communities. Five years later, in 1536, came another statute.[4] This
described previous acts as defective because they had made no
effective provision for the impotent poor and ordered all parish
and municipal authorities to assume responsibility for the impotent poor in their districts so that they would not have to beg.
Unfortunately, however, this act was itself unsuccessful as it made
no adequate provision for the financing and administration of such
relief. All it did was to authorize the collection of voluntary alms.

Despite the provisions for the impotent poor in the acts of 1531
and 1536 it does seem likely that throughout the first half of the
sixteenth century the main concern of the government was with
the problem of able-bodied vagrants. This is suggested by the
savage Edwardian statute of 1547[5] which introduced really fero-

---

[1] The best general discussion of Tudor legislation on the poor is E. M.
Leonard, *The Early History of English Poor Relief* (Cambridge, 1900). The main
weakness of this book is its inadequate treatment of the enforcement of the poor
law, which can, however, be studied in W. K. Jordan's important work,
Philanthropy in England 1480–1660 (1959)

[2] 11 Henry vii, c. 2.

[3] 22 Henry viii, c. 12.

[4] 27 Henry viii, c. 25.

[5] 1 Edward vi, c. 6.

cious penalties against the vagrant poor, prescribing servitude for two years upon first conviction, and lifelong slavery or even death for those who proved intractable. This act was so severe, however, that it was repealed in 1550, when the statute of 1531 was brought into force again.

The next law which must be noticed, that of 1552,[1] was concerned mainly with the collection of funds for the relief of the impotent poor. It provided a hint of the compulsion which was to be applied in Elizabeth's reign. Any person who had the means to make a voluntary contribution for poor relief, but who refused to do so, was to be exhorted by his local parson. If he still refused he was to be sent to the bishop who would try to 'induce and persuade him . . . by charitable ways and means'.

The position at the accession of Elizabeth, as far as national legislation is concerned, was, therefore, that some distinction had already been made in principle between vagabonds and the deserving poor. Vagabonds were to be whipped, the deserving poor were to be given relief in their own localities. Unfortunately the provisions for the relief of the deserving poor tended to remain dead letters until people could be compelled to pay for their support. That compulsion came in Elizabeth's reign.

The second base on which Elizabeth's national system was founded was the work undertaken by different towns to deal with the problem of their own vagrants and poor. Until the 1570s such measures by municipal authorities probably made more important contributions to the problems of poor relief than parliamentary legislation on the subject. Three of the most important towns which took such action were London, Ipswich and Norwich.[2] A compulsory assessed poor rate was instituted in London in 1547, the first time an obligatory tax was levied for the support of the poor, and twenty-five years before Parliament introduced compulsion and assessment on a national scale. Moreover, between 1544 and 1557 four institutions were organized in London for the relief or punishment of the poor: Christ's hospital, for orphan children; St. Bartholomew's and St. Thomas's hospitals, for the sick, aged and impotent poor; and Bridewell, for the punishment and training of rogues and vagabonds. In

[1] 5 & 6 Edward vi, c. 2.

[2] E. M. Leonard, *The Early History of English Poor Relief*, pp. 23–40 (London), pp. 42–3 (Ipswich), pp. 101–7 (Norwich).

1557, fifteen years before the national system of 1572, compulsory assessments for the upkeep of the poor were instituted in Ipswich. Any inhabitant who refused to pay was to be punished at the discretion of the town bailiff. In 1569 a municipal hospital was established and named Christ's hospital. It combined the functions of the four London hospitals, being a house of correction for rogues and vagabonds as well as a place of asylum for the old and a training school for the young. The third town, Norwich, established in 1570 and 1571 an extremely comprehensive system of poor relief which succeeded so well that its fame spread to all parts of the country, and Archbishop Parker asked specially for information about it. In 1570 there were more than 2,000 beggars in Norwich, many of whom would not work at all. They became wasteful and threw away the food given to them. In short they were a scandal to the town. In that year, therefore, an elaborate census of all the poor was taken and orders were drawn up for their relief. Norwich seems to have first instituted compulsory fixed contributions for poor relief in the 1560s but now in 1570 a new assessment was made and the contributions were in many cases considerably increased. Distinctions were carefully drawn between the different categories of poor: idle vagabonds; those who were willing to work; the impotent poor; and pauper children. Each category was to receive different treatment. These orders were put into force about May 1571 and a year later the town authorities were able to report that they had been a great success. Work had been provided for the poor who were able to undertake it and the disorderly vagrants who had resorted to the town in such numbers before 1570 had almost ceased to trouble it.

These municipal measures as well as the legislation of early Tudor parliaments must be borne in mind in any discussion of the system of poor relief instituted in the later sixteenth century.

The first Elizabethan act dealing with the poor, that of 1563,[1] applied, for the first time, compulsion on a national scale to the collection of funds for poor relief. Those who refused to contribute even after they had been exhorted by their bishop were to be summoned before the local J.P.s at the next quarter sessions, where a tax was to be levied upon them. If they defaulted, then they were to be sent to prison until payment was made. It is important

[1] 5 Eliz., c.3.

to stress that this act did not enforce payment of an *assessed* sum on all. Those who made voluntary contributions were still free to give as much and presumably therefore as little as they liked.

This, however, was changed in the next act, that of 1572.[1] The act of 1572 is a very important one as it dealt with both vagrancy and the impotent poor and summed up the experience of the past generation in tackling these problems. It defined as vagrants all able-bodied men without land or master who could not explain the source of their livelihood and also certain classes of men, such as peddlars, tinkers and minstrels, who had all too often proved to be vagrants. Having made this careful definition the law came down very heavily on vagrancy, which was outlawed under pain of whipping and boring through the ear for a first offence. For further offences penalties were much stiffer. Indeed for a third offence the vagrant was to be punished by death. There is evidence that this savage provision was carried out. Men and women were hanged for vagrancy in Elizabeth's reign.[2]

The act was, however, very careful to separate vagabonds from the deserving poor, who were defined as the impotent and aged. These were to be provided with relief and the justices of the peace and other local officials were ordered to raise money for this purpose by taxing, at a specific rate, all the inhabitants of their districts who were able to pay. Anyone who refused to contribute the assessed sum was to be imprisoned. The act also provided for the appointment of overseers of the poor in each parish.

From 1572 onwards, therefore, all the inhabitants of the country who had the means to do so were legally liable to pay *fixed* rates for the upkeep of the poor. This is the great achievement of the 1572 act, it recognized once and for all that the problem of the poor was a national problem and that everyone should be obliged to contribute towards its solution. On the other hand, the act did have two weaknesses. It provided that the justices and local officials were to levy poor rates in their 'districts' without defining these districts clearly and without providing for one district to go to the help of another if the need arose. These deficiencies were to be remedied in the 1598 act. Also, although the 1572 statute did make a distinction between vagabonds and

[1] 14 Eliz., c. 5.

[2] E. M. Leonard, *The Early History of English Poor Relief*, 70, note 2.

the deserving poor, it defined the latter merely as the impotent
and the aged. In other words it did not recognize the undoubted
fact that there were able-bodied men who were genuinely seeking
work which was not to be found. By the 1572 statute such men
would merely be classed as vagrants and would be subject to
the severe penalties already described. It was not until the acts
of 1576 and 1598 that provision was made for the able-bodied
who were anxious for work but unable to find it.

Such provision was made by implication only in the 1576 act,[1]
which ordered that raw materials such as wool, flax and iron
were to be maintained in every city, borough and market town
so that vagrants could be compelled to work and so that 'other
poor and needy persons being willing to work may be set on
work'. This was the last important measure on the poor before
the great legislation of 1598. The date of that legislation is largely
explained by the severe economic crisis which began in England
in 1594.[2] In that year and for the four following years there was
heavy and unseasonable rain. As a result there were five bad
harvests in succession, and these at a time when the economy was,
in any event, strained because of the war with Spain. The worst
year was 1596 when conditions were so bad that several regions
were actually threatened by famine. As a result of this situation
there was, of course, a great increase in the problems of vagrancy
and poverty. It became very plain in these years that there were
many able-bodied and wholly responsible men in both town and
country who were desperately anxious to work but for whom
work was simply not available. The harsh realities of the economic
situation had in fact made it crystal clear that there were three
main classes of poor: the vagrants; the able-bodied who were
genuinely unemployed; and the impotent poor. This was
recognized in the legislation of 1598.

In his discussion of that legislation, Sir John Neale has shown[3]
quite clearly that it was the result not of government initiative,
but of the initiative of the Commons themselves. The government
certainly approved, otherwise the new acts would never have
reached the statute book, but the fact remains that the lead was
given by members of the Commons, which was, of course,

[1] 18 Eliz., c. 3.
[2] On the economic and social crisis of 1594–98 see Cheyney, ii, pp. 3–36.
[3] Neale, *Parliaments*, ii, pp. 337–48.

composed mainly of country gentlemen who were intimately in touch with the distressing state of their localities.

Of the two main acts of 1598 dealing with the problems of vagrancy and the poor one was entitled 'An act for the punishment of rogues, vagabonds and sturdy beggars'.[1] This carefully defined vagabondage and then provided for the severe punishment of vagrants, who were to be whipped till their bodies were bloody and then returned to the parish of their birth or legal residence where they were first of all to be sent to the local gaol or house of correction and later were to be placed in service or in an almshouse. The other great statute of 1598, the most important piece of social legislation of that year, 'An act for the relief of the poor',[2] provided that in every parish the churchwardens and four other substantial householders should act as overseers of the poor. A compulsory rate was to be levied in each parish to provide relief for those poor people who were unable to work because of age or infirmity and also to buy a stock of commodities on which the able-bodied poor could work. The act, therefore, recognized clearly and unequivocally the fact of unemployment, the existence of a group of able-bodied poor who were willing to work but unable to find work and, moreover, by its order for the provision of raw materials it provided work for such people. If any parish was unable to raise by taxation the sums necessary for the relief of its own poor, then the required rates were to be spread over the hundred and, if necessary, over the county. The justices of the peace were given general oversight of the statute.

This act remained the basis of the system of English poor relief until the passing of the Poor Law Amendment Act of 1834. The act of 1601,[3] sometimes cited as the culmination of the Elizabethan legislation, was actually a re-enactment, with very slight alterations, of the 1598 statute.

This discusion of the Tudor statutes on the poor has shown quite clearly that the legislation had two different aspects. On the one hand it clearly reflected the determination of the governing classes – a determination continuous throughout the sixteenth century – to preserve law and order by the punishment and, if possible, by the suppression of vagrancy. On the other hand it also

[1] 39 Eliz., c. 4.
[2] 39 Eliz., c. 3.
[3] 43 Eliz., c. 2.

showed, in the Elizabethan period at least, the real and growing concern of the government and upper classes for the welfare of the genuinely poor and unfortunate. On the technical side one can see two great achievements in the Elizabethan legislation. First of all there was the institution of a compulsory poor rate and the creation of a system for its imposition, collection and administration. Here the important acts were those of 1563, 1572 and 1598, each of which was a development of and improvement on previous legislation. Secondly, there was the drawing of a workable and realistic distinction between the three main classes of poor: those who would not work – the vagabonds; those who could not work – the aged and infirm poor and pauper children; and those who wanted to work but could not find jobs – the unemployed. The beginnings of this distinction went back as far as Henry VIII's statute of 1531, but the really important acts here were those of 1572, 1576 and 1598. As already noted, the government did not take the lead in the debates and discussions which preceded the statutes of 1598, but it does seem to have taken the initiative in introducing most of the legislation on the poor. Despite this fact, however, it must not be given credit for any original ideas on the problems of poverty. All the ideas contained in the Elizabethan legislation were anticipated in the measures taken by the towns, notably London and Norwich.

Discussion of the content of the Elizabethan poor law is important but, of course, it was one thing to put legislation on the statute book and quite another to see that it was effectively enforced. Professor W. K. Jordan has recently examined the administration of the law, both in the period after the 1572 act, which instituted a compulsory poor rate on a national scale, and in the years after the 1598 act, which made much more elaborate provisions for the assessment of the rate. It seems from his work that, in both periods, it was only when local disaster struck, whether because of bad harvests or the outbreak of plague, that the responsible authorities resorted to the imposition of rates. It seems clear, in fact, that local authorities regarded rates as an emergency measure to tide the community over a period of crisis. Moreover, the central government seems to have made no sustained effort before the 1630s to enforce the legislation in the localities. It was, on the whole, quite happy to see the local communities resolving their problems in their own way, resorting to a poor rate in times of emergency, neglecting to impose it at other times. In fact Jordan has calculated that throughout England during the years 1560 to 1600 under £12,000 was disbursed in poor relief as a result of local taxation. On the other hand during this same period, in ten English counties, £174,000 was given by private charity for the relief of the poor.[1] These figures are most important. They show quite clearly that during the entire Elizabethan period the state's contribution to poor relief was entirely subordinate to private donations. England during Elizabeth's reign was still a very long way from being a welfare state.

No less important than the poor law in the social history of the reign was the statute of artificers of 1563.[2] This immensely long act, containing forty clauses and well over 8,000 words, attempted to regulate in detail the lives and occupations of the great majority of the Queen's subjects. Notably, it dealt with their choice of work, with the terms of their training, and with their wages. It provided that all males between the ages of twelve and sixty who were not exempt on one of several carefully defined grounds, were to work as agricultural labourers. This part of the act reflected the government's and Parliament's concern with the problem of vagabondage – all able-bodied men were to work – and their determination to ensure an adequate supply of agricultural labour – the able-bodied unemployed were directed to work on the land.

The statute also provided that from 1563 onwards no one was to be allowed to engage in any craft unless he had served an apprenticeship of at least seven years at that craft. The seven years' apprenticeship period was not a complete innovation, it was already the rule in London and in some other towns. What the 1563 act did was to make the rule applicable in all towns and in rural districts as well, thus generalizing it throughout the country. Two motives can be seen behind this. One was a desire to secure high standards of workmanship. This reflected a concern for the interests of the consumer, a concern which was not without justification, as it seems clear that some craftsmen who had previously served shorter terms of apprenticeship, perhaps as little as two years, were neither able to produce efficient work

---

[1] W. K. Jordan, *Philanthropy in England*, pp. 126–35.
[2] 5 Eliz., c. 5.

themselves nor to train others properly. Secondly, there was the desire to confine industry as rigidly as possible within the gild system. The seven years rule served this purpose. It not only introduced uniformity throughout the country, but clearly provided a barrier to change of occupation: a man who had spent seven years learning one craft was hardly likely to go off and spend seven years learning another. The apprenticeship clauses, in fact, reflected to a considerable extent the determination of the governing classes, in the depression conditions of the 1560s, to restrict and control the economy.

The third major set of provisions in the act dealt with wage rates. These highly paternalistic clauses ordered the justices of the peace in the shires and magistrates in the towns to compile annually and enforce continuously a set of wage rates for every occupation practised within their jurisdictions. Such assessment of wages by J.P.s was not, of course, new. The duty had first been imposed in the 14th century and in theory it had been lifted only during one or two short intervals since that date. In fact by 1563 such assessments had long since ceased to be made with any regularity.

Discussion of the terms of the statute reminds us that until recently historians interpreting it had at least one piece of common ground, all accepted it as a unitary thing, the work of the central government. In a recent article,[1] however, Professor S. T. Bindoff has shown that the story is much more complicated than that. It is now clear that the final act consists of two parts, an original government bill and the Commons amendments of and additions to that bill. The government's original bill, of between eighteen and twenty-one clauses, dealt, among other things, with wage assessments and compulsory labour in agriculture, although its provisions on these matters were amended in the Lower House. The Commons, as well as amending the original bill, added the clauses concerning compulsory seven years apprenticeships in all urban and rural crafts, the whole emerging as a much enlarged act of forty clauses. This action of the Commons is of undoubted importance. It redressed the balance of the original bill which had emphasized the importance of agriculture, while neglecting industry. Professor Bindoff con-

[1] S. T. Bindoff, 'The Making of the Statute of Artificers', *Elizabethan Government and Society*, pp. 56–94.

cludes, therefore, that whatever was forward-looking in the statute it owed to the House of Commons and not to the government. This is certainly true up to a point: the Commons by adding the seven years apprenticeship clauses for industrial workers showed that they realized the growing significance of industry in the national economy. On the other hand the *content* of these apprenticeship clauses, with their emphasis on restriction and control, suggests an attempt to limit industrial expansion – hardly a far-sighted policy.

It was one thing to pass the statute of artificers, quite another, as in the case of the poor law, to enforce it. Evidence for the enforcement of the 1563 statute is, on the whole, scattered, scanty and difficult to interpret. This is the case, for example, as far as the wage assessment clauses of the act are concerned.[1] On the other hand the enforcement of the apprenticeship clauses has been studied in great detail, on the basis of the prosecutions which took place for breaches in them.[2] These prosecutions were of two types, those brought by public servants, and those instigated by private persons. Mrs. Davies has calculated that in the period 1563–1642 less than five per cent of the total recorded number of prosecutions were brought by public authorities, although the true proportion of public to private prosecutions may have been in the region of one to five. The great majority of such public prosecutions were ineffective. She concludes that the enforcement of apprenticeship was neglected by both central and local government. The majority of private prosecutions, most of which were brought by professional informers, seem also to have been ineffective in enforcing the law.[3]

The ineffective enforcement of both the statute of artificers and the poor law brings home one of the notable features of Elizabethan government, the contrast which often existed between the legislation which was theoretically in force and the actual situation in the country. Elizabethan laws were frequently honoured as much in the breach as in the observance.

[1] On these see R. H. Tawney, 'The assessment of wages in England by the justices of the peace', *Vierteljahrschr. f. Sozial – und Wirtschaftsgesch*, xi (1913), pp. 307–37, 533–64; R. K. Kelsall *Wage Regulation under the Statute of Artificers*, (1938).
[2] M. R. G. Davies, *The Enforcement of English Apprenticeship 1563–1642*, (Cambridge, Massachusetts, 1956).
[3] *Ibid.*, 17, 143–4, 244, 266.

Another lesson, and one which can usefully sum up this discussion of economic and social policy, is that Elizabeth's government did not think primarily in economic terms at all. Its main aims were to preserve order and secure the defence of the realm, and much of the economic legislation of the period reflected these basic aims. Again, some economic measures were, from the government's point of view, a means of raising revenue for itself or its servants. It is true that the government did have a genuine paternalistic concern for the welfare of the people, but that concern might always be modified by the primary needs of defence and the preservation of order as well as by the exigencies of the actual economic situation. We have seen some of these themes illustrated in the statute of artificers and in the legislation on the poor. Clearly it would be wrong to see the Elizabethan government with a planned economic policy – it simply did not think in these terms. It might be nearer the truth to see Elizabethan economic legislation as a series of unplanned reactions to specific problems which thrust themselves upon the government and the governing classes. On the other hand this body of economic legislation does have a certain coherence, and what gives it that coherence is the fact that it reflects certain assumptions which were commonplaces to any sixteenth-century government: the need to preserve order, defend the realm, raise money, and promote subjects' welfare – these assumptions would be in the mind of any Elizabethan statesman or any member of the Elizabethan House of Commons who was drafting or considering a piece of legislation, economic or otherwise.

CHAPTER SEVEN

Local Government

I⊤ is difficult today, in an age of ever-increasing centralization, to appreciate the enormous importance of the agencies of local government in sixteenth-century England. In the Elizabethan period most of the population did not come into direct contact with the central authorities at all. For the great majority of the Queen's subjects it was local officials, expecially the justices of the peace, who determined their fates. When one remembers in addition the strength of local patriotism at the time – an Elizabethan who referred to his 'country' very often meant his native shire rather than England as a whole – it becomes clear that the details of county administration must occupy a most significant place in any account of sixteenth-century government.

It is commonplace, when discussing Elizabethan local government, to emphasize on the one hand the growing importance of the lords lieutenant and justices of the peace and to stress on the other the comparatively limited significance of the sheriff, the man who had been the most important medieval official in the shires, but whose power had been greatly reduced during the later middle ages and declined still further in the course of the sixteenth century. It should be emphasized, nevertheless, that this reduction in the sheriff's real authority did not mean an equivalent diminution of his load of work. In the sixteenth century he still presided over the monthly meetings of the county court, where minor civil suits were heard, and he had duties in connection with the meetings of the courts of assize and quarter sessions: the empanelling of juries, the production of prisoners, the execution of sentences. He was responsible for seeing that all royal writs addressed to persons within the county reached their correct destination, a large task since such writs were very numerous, and he also had to collect and account for certain ancient, and by the sixteenth century, unimportant forms of royal taxation. These heavy administrative and judicial responsibilities imposed in return for limited power, go far to explain why Elizabethan gentlemen were often reluctant to accept a sheriffdom, even though the office lasted for only one year. Equally important in making the position unattractive was the expense which it entailed. A sheriff was entitled to fees for the delivery of writs and the performance of various other duties, but these were usually calculated in pence or at most in shillings whereas his expenses came to hundreds of pounds. In a typical county the sheriff paid out a total of over £100 in fees for entry into and for leaving office and for the settlement of his accounts at the Exchequer. He also had to pay personally the salary of his undersheriff, which could amount to several hundred pounds, and his heaviest bill of all often came from his responsibilities for hospitality to the Queen, foreign ambassadors, the justices of assize, and other distinguished visitors who entered his shire.[1]

There is no doubt in fact that a sheriff's office in the Elizabethan period was generally a burdensome and expensive honour without the compensation of effective power. The exception was when a man's sheriffdom coincided with a year of parliamentary elections. In the election of knights of the shire a sheriff came into his own. He presided at the meeting of the county court where the election was held, he could manipulate the proceedings in a great variety of ways, he declared the result, and he sent the return – the official evidence of election – to Chancery. In fact the sheriff was the key official in the whole procedure, and was often prepared to resort to the most ingenious and disreputable tricks to get his favoured candidates elected. Reading Sir John Neale's account[2] of some of these tricks it is difficult to avoid the conclusion that on such occasions sheriffs were determined to push their authority to the very limit. It was the only chance they had of exercising real power, and they were determined not to miss it.

The decline of the sheriff inevitably left something of a vacuum in local government but the Tudors created a new official, the lord lieutenant, who soon filled at least part of the gap. The office of lord lieutenant, essentially military in character, arose out of the local emergencies and dangers of the Reformation years, though only its tentative beginnings can be seen during the

[1] Cheyney, ii, pp. 344-58.
[2] Neale, *Commons*, p. 77ff.

reign of Henry VIII. For a time after 1549, however, the central government showed a much wider conception of the possibilities of the office. In each of the last four years of Edward VI's reign lieutenants were sent into many counties. Indeed it looks as though Northumberland contemplated making the lieutenancy a permanent part of the English administrative system. Mary, however, did not follow the precedents of her brother's reign and between 1553 and 1558 lieutenants were appointed only at irregular intervals and for particular reasons.[1]

During the first thirty or so years of her rule Elizabeth followed the same policy as her sister in the appointment of lieutenants. In every one of these years, except 1561, lieutenants were appointed for some counties, but stress was always laid on the fact that the position was to be regarded as temporary and was only granted for a special reason; during these years commissions of lieutenancy were terminated as soon as the trouble which had necessitated their issue had been overcome.[2] In the 1580s, however, the years immediately before and after the Spanish Armada, there were significant developments in the history of the lieutenancy, developments which marked an important stage on the way to making the office a permanent fixture in the administration and which at the same time led to greatly increased importance for the lieutenants' deputies. News of Philip II's invasion preparations led to the issue between 1585 and 1587 of commissions of lieutenancy for nearly all the counties of England and the continuing threat from Spain even after the defeat of the Armada in 1588 meant that the new lieutenants were allowed to retain their posts for the rest of their lives. Lieutenants were usually peers and often privy councillors as well and might be responsible for more than one shire. In 1595, for example, there were seventeen lieutenants in charge of twenty-nine counties. In the past, when they had been appointed for only a few months in times of emergency, they had been able to remain on the spot in their areas of responsibility as long as their commissions lasted. After 1588, however, with the lieutenants holding office continuously for years, the situation was completely altered. Great officers of state like Burghley and Howard of Effingham, both of whom were lieutenants in the post Armada years, could not possibly stay away

[1] G. Scott Thomson, *Lords Lieutenant in the Sixteenth Century*, (1923), pp. 14–42.
[2] *Ibid.*, p. 46.

from Court for long stretches at a time. In these circumstances the work of the lieutenants came more and more, during the last fifteen years of the reign, to be done by deputies.[1]

Deputy lieutenants first appear as recognized officials early in Elizabeth's reign. They were appointed in accordance with special clauses in a lieutenant's commission which gave him the power to confer letters of deputation on certain of the gentry nominated by the Crown within his district. The Queen and her ministers sometimes nominated without consulting the lieutenant, but in the majority of cases the latter seems to have taken the initiative, suggesting names from among the local justices of the peace. There seems to have been no fixed rule as to the number of deputies allowed. The determining factor was probably the requirements of the lieutenant himself: the Earl of Bath had as many as six deputies for Devonshire in the 1580s. Lieutenants who had charge of more than one shire could not, however, appoint deputies to assist them throughout the entire area of their jurisdiction. Deputy lieutenants were always officials of a single county, appointed to act within that county alone. Lieutenants in control of several shires therefore had different deputies for each.[2]

The duties of lieutenants remained under Elizabeth, as they had begun under her father, primarily military. Lieutenants were responsible for the annual assembling, inspection and training for military service of a number of men within the county or counties under their control. These musters, as they were called, were held each summer and were very unpopular as they interfered with the general routine of country life. Throughout Elizabeth's reign many shirked their duty of attendance at musters, a duty which theoretically fell on all men between the ages of sixteen and sixty. From these a sufficient number of the most able-bodied were selected to be armed and trained. Full details of their names and equipment were kept in muster books which existed for each county and which were frequently called in for inspection by the Privy Council. Two paid officials, a

[1] *Ibid.*, pp. 42–59, 68; Cheyney, ii, p. 362.
[2] G. Scott Thomson, *Lords Lieutenant in the Sixteenth Century*, pp. 60–67; 'The Origin and Growth of the Office of Deputy-Lieutenant', *Transactions of the Royal Historical Society*, 4th series, v, pp. 153–6.

muster master and a provost marshal, existed to help with the
military organization of each shire. The former was responsible
for the detailed inspection of the men, horses and armour, the
latter was in charge of discipline, both under the general authority of the lieutenant himself, who carried out the annual muster
personally or through his deputies. Where there was no lieutenant
the job was done by commissioners for musters appointed by the
Crown. The unpopularity of the musters and the consequent
difficulties in finding the required number of men and the
necessary amount of equipment must at times have driven
lieutenants nearly to distraction, especially during the last fifteen
or so years of the reign, when they were ordered to raise levies
for service in the Low Countries or northern France. Men who
had had little desire to attend musters which were specifically
intended to secure the defence of their homeland had even less
enthusiasm for those which were summoned partly to secure
troops for overseas service. Large numbers did not attend at all,
and of those who did and were impressed by the harassed lieutenants and their officials, many deserted, from the musters themselves, from the ports of embarkation, and from the armies in
France and the Netherlands.[1]

Lieutenants' military tasks, difficult and demanding, were not
their only duties. They and their deputies were also responsible
for the collection of loans, which were raised by the Crown at
intervals to meet extraordinary expenses. On such occasions they
were required to furnish lists of the men of substance within their
jurisdictions, together with estimates of how much each might be
expected to pay; then to supervise the distribution to individuals
of royal letters of privy seal demanding the loan of a fixed sum;
and finally to persuade recalcitrant gentlemen to pay up.
Lieutenants also had responsibilities for the supervision of
recusants and exercised some oversight of economic regulations
in their counties, enforcing orders concerning abstention from
meat in Lent, organizing the supply of foodstuffs for the navy
and superintending the distribution of grain in times of scarcity.[2]

Lieutenants were under the direct and constant supervision
of the Privy Council. They received detailed instructions from
the Council Board and were expected to make equally full reports

[1] G. Scott Thomson, *Lords Lieutenant in the Sixteenth Century*, pp. 84-94, 107-116.
[2] *Ibid.*, pp. 117-40.

to it. The dignity of their office and their own personal standing ensured that such reports would receive careful consideration. They thus formed a vital link between the central government and the localities, presenting the views of their districts to the Council and conveying its opinions and orders to their shires. Relations between Council and lieutenants seem to have been generally satisfactory during the reign. Council letters to lieutenants contain reproofs and searching criticisms but it was never necessary to remove a lieutenant from office: a commentary on the excellence of the Queen's or perhaps Burghley's choice of men. Deputies were not, however, so fortunate. Several were dismissed and replaced, 'for the better service of her Majesty'.[1]

Lieutenants and their deputies were thus burdened with a number of arduous duties and were closely supervised by the Council. By way of compensation a lieutenant was, by the end of Elizabeth's reign, almost certainly the chief man of the counties over which he held sway. The office was not yet a permanent one – many of the lieutenants appointed in the 1580s were not replaced when they died – and much water was to flow under the bridge before the lieutenant reached his full eighteenth-century stature as a permanent officer identified with a single county.[2] Nevertheless the creation of the office of lord lieutenant with all its contemporary uses and future potentialities was the work of Tudor sovereigns and ministers, particularly of Queen Elizabeth and her councillors. That was a notable achievement in local government.

The lord and deputy lieutenants stood at the apex of county administration. Beneath them were the justices of the peace, the key figures in local government. The office of J.P. was, of course, a medieval creation, but during the sixteenth century there was a great increase in the numbers and work of the justices. At the beginning of the Tudor period there were, on average, less than ten J.P.s per shire, but by the middle of Elizabeth's reign the average was perhaps forty or fifty. In 1580 there were in all 1,738 J.P.s in England, the smallest number in any county being in Rutland where there were thirteen, and the largest in Kent where there were eighty-three. In Wiltshire the number of justices increased from thirty in 1562 to fifty-two in 1600 and this pattern was repeated in Norfolk where there were thirty-seven at

[1] *Ibid.*, pp. 73–7.
[2] *Ibid.*, pp. 141–2.

the beginning of Elizabeth's reign and sixty-one in 1602. It is tempting to see the principal reason for this great inflation in numbers in the vastly increased amount of work which J.P.s were required to shoulder during the Tudor period. It would seem sensible to conclude that more work meant the need for more justices. This argument should not be pushed too far. Throughout the Elizabethan period only a minority of J.P.s seem to have been active in any county and the initiative in increasing the size of the commissions of the peace seems to have come from the local gentry rather than from the Crown, which constantly tried to reduce the number of justices in the interests of more efficient administration. The persistence of the local gentry and the Crown's failure to secure more than very temporary reductions in the size of the commissions suggest that the principal reason for the greatly increased numbers was a social one. It was a mark of prestige to be a justice of the peace. To be left out of the ranks might be regarded as an indignity, an affront to one's family. Hence the clamour for seats on the bench.[1]

The increase in the volume of the justices' work can be illustrated by discussing the growing number of statutes which required J.P.s' assistance for their enforcement. William Lambarde, in the 1599 edition of his *Eirenarcha*, the most famous Tudor treatise on the justices' office, listed 306 such statutes. Of these only 133 predated 1485, sixty were made between 1485 and 1547, thirty-eight belonged to the reigns of Edward VI and Mary, and seventy-five were passed in Elizabeth's reign between 1559 and 1597.[2] Although some of these statutes were of limited significance from the justices' point of view others contained complex and vitally important provisions. This was especially true of the Elizabethan statutes dealing with apprenticeship, the poor and vagrancy, the famous Elizabethan social legislation which, as previously pointed out,[3] imposed heavy burdens on the J.P.s.

This list of statutes brings home the vast number of administrative tasks imposed upon justices by the end of the Tudor period, but it represents only one source of their powers and duties. The

[1] G. R. Elton, *The Tudor Constitution*, p. 453; Cheyney, ii, pp. 313–14; A. H. Smith, 'The Elizabethan Gentry of Norfolk: office-holding and faction', (London University Ph.D. thesis, 1959), pp. 80, 328; *The Victoria History of the Counties of England, Wiltshire*, v (1957), p. 89.

[2] W. Lambarde, *Eirenarcha* (1599 edition), p. 608ff.

[3] See chapter 6.

other, the commission of the peace, which emphasized the judicial as opposed to the administrative aspects of the justices' office, was issued each year. By the end of the middle ages this commission had assumed a fixed form which remained for the greater part of the Tudor period, although it became increasingly unsatisfactory because of the increase in the J.P.s work. In 1590, however, it was thoroughly revised and remained in force in this new form for over 300 years. In the new form (and here only the broadest summary is possible) the commission authorized the justices to enforce all statutes concerning the peace; gave them powers to inquire by sworn inquest into a variety of felonies and offences at common and statute law; gave them the right to hear and determine a variety of cases; and instructed them to hold regular sessions for their work.[1]

Turning from the sources of the justices' authority to their organization for work, we cannot do better than follow Lambarde, who divided his classic study of the J.P.s into four books. The first of these gives a general view of the office of justice of the peace, the second sets out the cases with which a single justice could deal, the third discusses those which required the attention of more than one justice but which could still be dealt with outside the sessions of the peace, the fourth deals with the sessions of the peace themselves.

The second book, dealing with the powers of a single justice, occupies 228 pages out of a total of 607,[2] which gives some idea of the range of authority wielded by a lone J.P. He had extensive criminal jurisdiction. In cases of breach of the peace he could commit the culprits to gaol; he could order sheriffs and bailiffs to search for thieves and robbers; he had powers under statutes relating to unlawful hunting and games, to tippling in ale-houses, to sanctuaries, to thefts of horses, and to the examination of felons, to mention only a few. Lambarde warned that a justice having in such cases 'the whole matter committed to himself alone, ought to be wary and circumspect, lest either he rashly condemn the guiltless or negligently suffer the guilty to escape', an ample commentary on the extent of the justice's powers and the possibility of their abuse.

In contrast to his extensive criminal jurisdiction a single justice's civil powers were small, being limited to the settlement

[1] G. R. Elton, *The Tudor Constitution*, pp. 453–4.
[2] W. Lambarde, *Eirenarcha*, pp. 74–302.

of disputes between masters and their servants and apprentices. He did, however, have considerable administrative authority, most of which stemmed from Tudor statutes, especially those dealing with vagrancy and the poor. In addition he had several responsibilities under the religious legislation of Elizabeth's reign. For example, he could fine offenders for non-attendance at church and if any person informed him of the delivery of a cross, picture or other 'superstitious' object from Rome and of the name and address of the deliverer he was required to report the matter to a member of the Privy Council.[1]

Lambarde's third book, dealing with the powers of two or more justices, occupies only fifty-nine pages,[2] and in fact the powers of two justices were similar in kind but different in degree to those of one acting alone. In criminal matters they could punish riots, bail prisoners, deal with offences under the statute of artificers, convict for offences under the game laws, make orders in respect of bastard children, and deal with those who evaded their obligations to make subsidy payments. Their civil jurisdiction, like that of a single justice, was very limited, but they had heavy administrative duties. They had many responsibilities in connection with the poor law: the appointment of overseers and the assessment of rates to relieve poor parishes are examples. They were also given control of the sheriffs and other older local officials. For example, they could examine sheriffs' books and the fines inflicted by them. Another of their duties was the licensing of ale-houses and they performed a number of miscellaneous tasks such as giving testimonials to servants who had been dismissed and supervising the accounts of hospitals.[3]

Three justices had even more extensive judicial and administrative authority, and it is clear that the work of J.P.s acting singly or in groups was essential to prevent the sessions of the peace being completely overrun with business. Nevertheless the principal work of the justices still centred on quarter sessions. It was only at these meetings that they could exercise all their powers, and the length of Lambarde's fourth book,[4] which describes the sessions of the peace in 243 pages, is a reflection of their importance.

[1] W. S. Holdsworth, *History of English Law*, iv, (3rd ed., 1924), pp. 138–40.

[2] W. Lambarde, *Eirenarcha*, pp. 303–62.

[3] W. S. Holdsworth, *History of English Law*, iv. pp. 140–42.

[4] W. Lambarde, *Eirenarcha*, pp. 363–606.

Quarter sessions, as the name implies, were held four times a year, though additional sessions were frequently called when the pressure of business made them necessary. All the justices of the county were supposed to be present but attendance was actually very irregular. In the west riding of Yorkshire between 1597 and 1600, for example, only six or eight J.P.s were usually present out of a total of fifty-seven. A meeting could continue for three consecutive days if this was found necessary, but in practice, and despite the pressure of business, sessions usually lasted only one day. The procedure was very different from the informal methods adopted when justices, acting singly or in small groups, dealt with the miscellaneous cases described above. Quarter sessions were conducted with all the organization and formality of an important judicial gathering and, besides the J.P.s themselves, required the attendance of the sheriff or his deputy to empanel juries and execute sentences; the gaoler, who had to produce his prisoners; all jurors and witnesses who had been summoned by the sheriff; all persons who had been bound over by individual justices to appear at quarter sessions; all high constables and bailiffs of hundreds; and the coroner.

Procedure was still medieval in form. Quarter sessions was a meeting between the justices of the peace and the whole county, represented by jurors, in which the latter, in answer to a specific list of questions, were required to provide the justices with information about persons guilty of crimes or offences against the law of Church or state. Offenders were then tried and punished. Quarter sessions did not have important civil jurisdiction and had no authority to hear cases involving treason, forgery and a few other great crimes. Otherwise, however, their criminal jurisdiction was hardly different from that of the royal courts at Westminster or the judges of assize. Justices in quarter sessions tried persons accused of murder, assault, burglary, witchcraft, disorderly conduct, cheating, keeping nuisances, violation of industrial laws, failure to attend church, religious dissent, vagrancy, and a host of other crimes and misdemeanours. Punishments on conviction were harsh in the extreme. The stocks was the mildest penalty available, floggings were very frequent, and offenders were occasionally sent to the galleys. Hanging was common. In Derbyshire, in the winter sessions of 1598, eighteen offenders were hanged out of sixty-five tried, and in the spring sessions the number was twelve out of forty-five. These figures are no doubt exceptional, but they do give a striking impression of the power of the justices in quarter sessions and the ruthlessness with which that power was sometimes exercised.

Meetings of quarter sessions were only partly judicial in character. The justices also used these occasions to take action on many administrative tasks which they could not or did not perform at other times: examples are the supervision of houses of correction, the fixing of wage rates, and the administration of some aspects of the poor law.[1]

Control over J.P.s was exercised by the Queen and the Privy Council. That control could not be *too* strict. Justices were unpaid and in the last resort the Crown relied almost completely on their voluntary co-operation to enforce its will in the localities. For example, in the Elizabethan period, the gentry were grossly underassessed for the payment of parliamentary subsidies. This was largely because the assessments were made by local commissioners, most of whom were J.P.s and themselves members of the gentry class. The Crown might and did complain about justices underassessing themselves in this way, but there was very little it could do when the whole class was involved. On the other hand it was dangerous for individual justices to oppose the Crown too often on *specific* matters. By doing so they ran the risk of being left out of the next commission of the peace. The Queen herself took a direct interest in the justices and their work and had no hesitation in ordering the removal of J.P.s who displeased her. In 1595, for example, she looked through the entire list of justices and indicated some names which she wished omitted from the next commission. Moreover, J.P.s were never allowed to forget the existence of the Privy Council, which bombarded them with a stream of specific requirements and commands, a stream which increased as the Elizabethan period progressed.[2]

Discussion so far has been concerned with local administration at county level, but other smaller units, notably the hundred and parish, also deserve attention. The hundred, or wapentake as it was known in seven of the northern and midland shires,

[1] Cheyney, ii, pp. 323–8, 331–4; W. S. Holdsworth, *History of English Law*, iv, pp. 142–4.

[2] F. C. Dietz, *English Public Finance 1558–1641*, pp. 384–8; Cheyney, ii, pp. 318, 336.

retained a considerable degree of administrative importance at
the end of the sixteenth century. The justices, when discharging
their multifarious duties, often tacitly organized themselves by
hundreds; the lord lieutenant and his deputies carried out their
musters hundred by hundred; and the hundred was a fundamental unit for purposes of royal taxation. Its chief officers were
the high constables, usually two for each hundred, who were
principally tax collectors, but also had military and police duties.[1]

Much more important than the hundred, however, was the
parish. This was originally a unit of ecclesiastical government,
but after the Reformation Tudor sovereigns began to use it as
part of the machinery of secular administration. During the
reigns of Henry VIII, Edward VI and Mary it was given various
responsibilities for poor relief and under Mary it was also made
responsible for the upkeep of highways. It was only in Elizabeth's
reign, however, that the parish achieved full status as a major
unit of local government. As we have seen, the Elizabethan
legislation on the poor gave it an organized machinery for raising
and administering a poor rate, and that machinery was rapidly
adopted for the collection of other dues, such as rates for the des-
truction of vermin and for the relief of prisoners and of disabled
soldiers and sailors. By 1603 the parish, with its ancient officials,
the constables and churchwardens, and its new executive staff of
surveyors of roads and overseers of the poor – both offices Tudor
creations – played a most significant role in the government of
England.[2]

It is right, when considering Elizabethan local government,
to concentrate on the country, but the towns must not be completely neglected. Borough governments differed one from another, but everywhere, in the Tudor period, the tendency was
towards closed corporations. Norwich had probably the most
liberal constitution of any Elizabethan town and even that was a
compromise between oligarchy and democracy. More typical
was Exeter, where the government was in the hands of a self-
perpetuating body of twenty-four who reserved all the chief
offices of power to themselves, while all the minor officials were
dependent upon the twenty-four for their appointments, for the

[1] Neale, *Commons*, pp. 21–2; Cheyney, ii, pp. 389–95.
[2] W. S. Holdsworth, *History of English Law*, iv, pp. 155–60; Cheyney, ii, pp.
400–415.

direction of their duties, and for their continuance in office.[1]

The picture so far presented has conveyed no impression of the importance of patronage and the significance of the clientage system in the English counties. Yet the tentacles of faction reached out over the countryside and exercised a profound influence on local life and on the government of the shires. No one has brought this out better than Dr. Hassell Smith in a recent unpublished study of Elizabethan Norfolk. The history of that county during the Queen's reign, he suggests, can be divided into two clearly defined periods; the years of the supremacy of the Duke of Norfolk, and the years after his execution in 1572. During the first period there is little doubt that the duke controlled the appointment of local government officials; this is not surprising in view of his unchallenged pre-eminence in the county. In the period after 1572, however, in the absence of any powerful nobleman, the county divided into factions, and by comparing the chronological sequence of their squabbles with the dates of the appointment and dismissal of J.P.s, sheriffs, and deputy lieutenants, a considerable correlation can be found between quarrels in the shire and appointments to the offices of local government. Between 1578 and the end of Elizabeth's reign eighty-two J.P.s were appointed in Norfolk and at least thirty-six of these appointments are explicable in terms of county factions. Moreover, the local faction struggles can account for the dismissal of some of the justices. Sixty-four Norfolk justices were removed at least once from the bench during Elizabeth's reign, and eighteen of these dismissals were the direct result of quarrels in the county. The picture is broadly similar with regard to sheriffs, deputy lieutenants, and commissioners for musters.[2] Dr. Hassell Smith's study thus demonstrates forcibly the intimate links which existed between county factions and local administration in sixteenth-century Norfolk. The situation in other counties cannot have been entirely dissimilar.

The existence of such factional conflicts does not, of course, obscure the significance of the creative changes which took place in the localities in the later sixteenth century: the very important

---

[1] A. L. Rowse, *The England of Elizabeth* (1950), pp. 173–5; W. T. MacCaffrey, *Exeter* (Cambridge, Massachusetts, 1958), pp. 29–31.

[2] A. H. Smith, 'The Elizabethan gentry of Norfolk: office-holding and faction' (London University Ph.D. thesis, 1959), pp. 329–31.

developments in the office of lord lieutenant, the creation of the position of deputy lieutenant, a great expansion in the work of the justices of the peace, and the establishment of the parish as a major unit in secular government. These changes, necessitated mainly by the continuing decline of the sheriff's authority, by pressing military problems, and above all by the passing of the Elizabethan social legislation, bear witness to the importance of the Queen's reign in the history of English local government.

CHAPTER EIGHT

Conclusion

THE term 'Tudor despotism' has disappeared from modern textbooks and historians are increasingly surprised that it could ever have been used. The theoretical limitations on the power of Tudor monarchs have, of course, always been recognized – their inability to make laws and impose taxes without the consent of Parliament – but it is only in comparatively recent years that the extent of the practical restrictions on their power has been generally appreciated.[1] Perhaps the most important of all these restrictions was the lack of a professional machinery for enforcing the royal will in the localities. In the absence of a local bureaucracy sixteenth-century English governments depended on the voluntary co-operation of the justices of the peace and that co-operation was only forthcoming if the orders of the government met with the general approval of the bulk of the local gentry, the men who dominated the bench. The failure of Elizabeth's government to suppress large-scale recusancy in Lancashire or to compel the local justices throughout the country to assess themselves at a reasonable rate for purposes of taxation reveals very clearly the limitations of its power: Elizabethan government was government by consent. Despite such exceptions, however, consent was generally forthcoming. The majority of the governing classes throughout the country were in broad agreement with most of the Queen's policies during her reign. That is one important reason why Elizabeth's government was, in the main, successful.

Successful government, of course, depended on control, vigour and sensible policies at the centre no less than on consent in the localities, and the Queen and her ministers provided these qualities, at least until the last decade of the reign. The Queen, through the pageantry of the royal court and through the

[1] In 1935 Professor C. H. Williams could still write a book entitled *The Making of the Tudor Despotism.*

frequent progresses on which she displayed her unique combination of dignity and familiarity, exploited the mystique of monarchy to serve the ends of government. On a more mundane level
her interventions in the details of everyday administration were
frequent enough to keep her ministers and officials on their toes,
but not too frequent to hamper the workings of the government
machine: the Queen never made the mistake of trying to do
everything herself. Her policies too served the country well for
the greater part of the reign. By her economy she husbanded her
meagre financial resources; by her moderation she reduced the
domestic political temperature, especially in the religious field;
by her conservative attitude to the foreign situation she generally
avoided reckless adventures abroad; and it is at least arguable
that her prevarication – her frequent inability to make up her
mind about important issues – enabled her to live with and
eventually even to solve many problems which active policies
might have brought to far less satisfactory conclusions.

The Queen, it is true, was lucky in her ministers: in the two
Cecils, Walsingham, Mildmay, Hatton and others she had servants of conspicuous ability and devotion to duty. But these men
were able to place their great talents at the service of the state
only because the Queen recognized their capacities and appointed
them to positions of responsibility. If the success of Elizabeth's
government is explained largely by the abilities of her ministers,
it must also be explained by the Queen's almost uncanny knack
of picking the right men for the job. Ministers, who performed
important individual roles, together formed the Privy Council,
and the significance of that body in the story of Elizabethan
government can hardly be overemphasized. It not only advised
the Queen on matters of policy but also supervised the entire
administration of the country, a task which it seems to have
performed with considerable efficiency in the Elizabethan period.
Internal administration and security also depended largely on
the secretary of state, who combined many of the responsibilities
of a modern home and foreign secretary. The potentialities of the
office were exploited to the full during the reign by a series of
able secretaries, among whom the Cecils and Walsingham were
pre-eminent.

The success of Elizabethan central government is also partly
explained by Elizabeth's relationship with her Parliaments and

by her management of patronage. Elizabethan Parliaments could be difficult and critical, but there was a fundamental harmony of outlook between the Queen and her faithful Commons which prevented difficulties from becoming too acute: both were dedicated to the preservation of Protestantism in England and a pro-protestant foreign policy, however much they might quarrel about details. Given these circumstances and the Queen's skilful management of the Lower House it is not surprising that the parliamentary history of the reign can be seen almost in terms of a romance between Crown and Commons. Indeed the passionate loyalty of the Elizabethan House of Commons to the Queen must have gone a long way towards ensuring the success of local government during the reign. Local government, as we have seen, was government by consent, and the memory of Elizabeth's personality and gracious speeches must have remained in the minds of country gentlemen when they returned from a session of Parliament to their localities. Such memories must at least have helped to secure their co-operation in the work of local administration.

The Queen's wise management of the patronage system was also an important factor in the success of her government. Her resolve never to limit her confidence and with it the control of patronage to a single minister or a single faction ensured that the Crown would never become the prisoner of its own servants and that royal bounty would be distributed through a number of channels. That policy succeeded until the 1590s when Essex's ambitions challenged its fundamental premise. Indeed, the 1590s saw important changes in many aspects of government. The situation described in the preceding paragraphs, with the Queen in firm control of a vigorous government following sensible policies, applies essentially to the early and high Elizabethan periods, the years before about 1590. During the 1590s, however, developments took place which both suggest the breakdown of the classic Elizabethan system and also, in many instances, presage developments in the early Stuart period. The 1590s will receive attention later, but first of all it may be illuminating to compare Elizabeth's government with the governments of the two great foreign states on which contemporary English opinion was primarily focused, France and Spain.

If the history of English government in the second half of the sixteenth century is, on the whole, a story of success, the history of French government in the same period is very clearly a story of failure. While Elizabeth succeeded in preserving internal peace in England, France was plagued from the 1560s until the 1590s by civil war. The reasons for that endemic domestic strife are numerous and complicated; the French Crown in the 1560s faced a series of religious, political, social and economic problems which made Elizabeth's difficulties seem slight by comparison. One reason does stand out above all others, however, in explaining the French government's almost total failure to deal with these problems: the weakness of the monarchy in personal terms. In theory a French king had much greater power than his English counterpart – he could, for example, issue laws and impose taxes on his own authority – but the efficient exercise of these powers was dependent upon the ability of the reigning sovereign. It was the misfortune of France in the later sixteenth century that, at a time when the country was faced with problems of unprecedented magnitude, the throne was occupied by three kings who were totally unfitted for the task. Francis II, who ruled from 1559 to 1560, ascended the throne as a sickly boy of fifteen; Charles IX (1560–74) became king at the age of nine; and Henry III, who occupied the throne between 1574 and 1589, was a psychiatrist's delight, a manic depressive who indulged alternately in the wildest excesses and the most extreme forms of repentance. The Queen Mother, Catherine de Medici, was the most important figure in French history during these three reigns, but her efforts to govern the country proved unsuccessful for a number of reasons; she faced enormous problems, her abilities were limited, her concern was focused upon her children rather than upon France, and, above all, she was not the sovereign. It was only after 1589 with Henry IV, a strong king, on the throne, that France began to recover. 'One fact is certain', wrote Professor Neale in his study of the French wars of religion, 'had France possessed such a king in 1559, or even later, its history would have been startlingly different'.[1] Comparison of French and English government during these years demonstrates with abundant clarity that the story of England's success and France's failure can be written largely in terms of the personalities and abilities of their rulers.

The story in Spain is very different from that in France. Philip

[1] J. E. Neale, *The Age of Catherine de Medici* (1943), p. 100.

II (1556–98) was firmly in control of his government throughout his long reign.[1] English historians have tended to regard Philip as a failure, citing the defeat of the Armada and his inability to retain control of the whole of the Netherlands in support of their views. Such a thesis – centred on northern Europe – reflects English parochialism rather than a dispassionate assessment of Philip's achievements. Regarded in broader terms he appears much more successful. It is true that he failed to conquer England and that he virtually lost the northern Netherlands, but he not only kept the rest of the vast empire which he had inherited from his father but passed it on to his successor greatly enlarged by the acquisition of Portugal and the Portuguese Empire. The extent of his dominions, a source of his strength, also gave rise to grave problems. Each of his different kingdoms had its own form of government – for example, Philip was absolute in Castile, a constitutional monarch in Aragon – and communications were so slow and difficult that royal orders could take a long time to reach the remoter parts of the empire. This last consideration helps to explain one of the characteristics of Philip's government which has been much criticized; its slowness. 'Your Majesty spends so long considering your undertakings', wrote Pope Pius V, 'that when the moment to perform them comes, the occasion has passed.' It is certainly true that Philip took a long time to make up his mind, but it must be remembered that once a decision was finally reached and dispatched it was very difficult to recall it. The difficulty of communications and the vastness of the empire meant that once the King had issued his commands he tended to become the servant rather than the master of events. In these circumstances it may be that his slowness, which, like Elizabeth's prevarication, at least gave difficulties a chance to resolve themselves, was not without its advantages.

Philip himself worked very hard at the business of government. There can surely never have been a more diligent monarch. Not only did he decide all matters of policy personally, but he virtually ran the entire administration of the Spanish Empire from his study. A mass of reports reached him from all corners of his dominions and he tried to deal with virtually all of these person-

[1] There are excellent brief accounts of Spanish government under Philip II in J. H. Elliott, *Imperial Spain 1469–1716* (1963), chapter 7, and J. Lynch, *Spain under the Habsburgs*, i (Oxford, 1964), chapter 6.

ally. The result was that he was always immersed in details. As
he was never able to distinguish between the important and the
trivial, he spent many hours on issues that could well have been
dealt with by officials. This determination to do everything
himself stemmed in part from the advice of his father Charles V,
who had told him never to trust anybody, and in part from his
own nature. It meant that he worked harder at the details of
government than Elizabeth ever did, but probably with less real
success. Elizabeth certainly never got submerged in minutiae and
thus had more time to consider broader aspects of policy. Moreover, Philip's constitutional inability to trust his advisers is in
striking contrast with Elizabeth's confidence in and loyalty to
her great ministers. There were no Burghleys or Walsinghams in
the Spain of Philip II.

Just as Philip had no great ministers, so also he lacked a
central administrative body for the whole of the Spanish Empire:
there was no institution in Spain comparable to the English Privy
Council. The Council of State, theoretically the highest of Philip's
councils, was merely an advisory body, and its importance even
in this field was very limited in view of the King's insistence on
keeping matters of policy in his own hands. There were other
councils, for example those for Castile, Italy, the Indies, and
Finance – the whole central government was organized on a
conciliar basis – but each had responsibilities only for the area
or field of its own jurisdiction. The Council of Castile, which was
probably the most important, was supposed to supervise the
administration of the Castilian kingdoms, but in practice it had
little time to devote to these responsibilities. This was because,
like the other councils, it combined administrative and judicial
functions and because the tendency in sixteenth-century Spain
was to regard government primarily in terms of jurisdiction – a
king's first duty was to do justice to his subjects. This meant that
all the councils tended to be overwhelmed with judicial business.
Their administrative duties suffered in consequence, and Philip,
with his conservative attitude towards the machinery of government, did little to help matters. It was not, for example, until 1598,
the very last year of his reign, that he divided the Council of
Castile into two departments, one for administrative and one for
judicial affairs. For most of the time he simply tried to fill the
administrative void left by his councils' other commitments by

applying himself with almost pathetic diligence to the details o government.

Of course, Philip had to have some link between himself and the councils. That link was provided by the royal secretaries. Each council had a secretary attached to it, and the King maintained liaison with the Council of State through his principal secretary who might be described as his secretary of state. The secretaries examined all incoming dispatches with the King and with his approval sent them to the appropriate council for attention. Although they were not themselves members of the councils, they attended meetings and drafted the *consultas*, the councils' reports to the King. Clearly a secretary occupied a key position at the centre of the administration, but the great potentialities of the office were not exploited in Philip's reign; it never approached the importance of the English secretaryship of state. With his ingrained suspicion of the motives of his servants the King firmly resisted any tendency for his secretaries to assume independent functions and responsibilities and they remained in the uneasy position of being much more than clerks but a good deal less than ministers. Some of them were able men, Antonio Perez very able. Perez tried, towards the end of his career as secretary, to act as a politician rather than an administrator, involving himself without authority in the affairs of the Netherlands and perhaps of Portugal as well. As a result he was dismissed in 1579.

During his career Perez had been an important member of the Eboli faction at Court, indeed after Eboli's death in 1573 he had become its leader. The field of faction and patronage is one area in which there were striking similarities between the English and Spanish systems of government. During the first twenty or so years of Philip's reign there were two great factions in Spain towards which councillors and officials tended to gravitate. One was led by the Duke of Alba, the other by the Prince of Eboli. The factions were divided on questions of foreign policy – just as the Leicester and Burghley factions on the English Privy Council were divided in the 1570s and 1580s – but they were also concerned with securing wealth and power for their members. As in England, money and influence could be procured by building up a system of clients through the distribution of royal patronage, which could, in turn, be obtained by the King's favour. Thus the struggle between the Alba and Eboli factions, just like the struggle in England between the followers of Leicester and Burghley, and later of Essex and Robert Cecil, was largely a contest for the control of patronage with its accompanying benefits.

If there were striking similarities between the workings of the Spanish and English patronage systems, there were very great differences in the local government of the two countries. In England, of course, local government depended essentially on the co-operation of the justices of the peace, unpaid members of the local gentry, who served on a voluntary basis. Unlike Elizabeth, Philip had, in Castile at least, the services of professional local administrators paid by the Crown, the *corregidores*. The office of *corregidor* dated from the fourteenth century, but it had only been generalized throughout Castile in 1480, when Ferdinand and Isabella appointed *corregidores* to all the chief towns. By Philip II's reign there were sixty-six *corregidores* in Castile, with both administrative and judicial responsibilities. Unlike English justices of the peace *corregidores* had no intimate connections with the localities to which they were appointed, and this, together with the fact that by the end of the sixteenth century their influence extended to virtually every corner of Castile, made them most effective instruments of the royal will.

The main impression one gets of Spanish government in the later sixteenth century is the extent of its dependence on the King's personal diligence. Spain depended even more on Philip than England did on Elizabeth. The latter had her great ministers and her Privy Council to help her in the formulation of policy and in administration. Philip, in constrast, relied almost wholly on himself not only in the making of policy but also in the task of keeping the cumbersome Spanish administrative machine moving.

Comparison between the Elizabethan governmental system and contemporary foreign governments may, however, be less illuminating than an attempt to compare Elizabeth's government with what preceded and what followed it in England. How did the Elizabethan system compare with the government of the early Stuarts? Was government and administration very different in 1600 than it had been in 1500? Dr. G. R. Elton has no doubts about the answer to the last question. In 1953, in his *Tudor Revolution in Government*, he advanced the view that the 1530s saw a rapid and almost complete transition from 'medieval' to 'modern' methods of government. Medieval government he equated with 'household' government: a governmental system where the mainspring of action was to be found in the royal household; modern government with 'bureaucratic' government: a system in which great departments of state were capable of carrying on the government of the country to a large extent independently of the monarch.

This thesis, founded upon detailed research among a large number of difficult sources, has provoked considerable discussion,[1] but has not gained universal acceptance. At least some medievalists, it seems, are unhappy with the description of medieval government as essentially 'household' government, and there are certainly early modern specialists who would not describe the governmental system of the late sixteenth and early seventeenth centuries as 'bureaucratic' without a good many more qualifications than Dr. Elton seems prepared to make. An important difficulty in accepting Elton's arguments arises from his failure to differentiate with sufficient clarity between government (the making and control of policy) and administration (the machinery by which policy is carried out). This was pointed out by Professor Wernham in 1956[2] and the distinction seems a vital one. The great difference between medieval and modern *government* is that in the middle ages (and indeed much later) policy was the responsibility of the Crown, whereas today it is the responsibility of the Crown's ministers. The story of the transition from medieval to modern forms of government is the story of how control of policy was taken out of the sovereign's hands and given instead to his ministers. That was a long process – the change was not complete until the nineteenth century – and the Tudor period does not represent a vital stage in the development. During the years 1500 to 1600 control of policy remained indubitably in the hands of the Crown.

Moreover, when we turn from government to *administration* it

---

[1] Dr. Elton has recently taken the opportunity of a debate in *Past and Present* with Drs. G. L. Harriss and Penry Williams to state that, while he would now modify his original thesis in several comparatively minor particulars, he stands by his fundamental interpretation as advanced in *The Tudor Revolution in Government*. For this debate see *Past and Present*, July 1963, December 1964, July 1965, and December 1965.

[2] *EHR*, lxxi (1956), pp. 93–4.

appears that the Elizabethan system combined elements of bureaucracy with informal arrangements on a fairly large scale. For example, during the period 1572 to 1598, when Burghley had formally ceased to be secretary of state, he continued to concern himself with the whole field of the country's foreign relations and used members of his private secretariat to assist him with such work. Indeed, examination of the private secretariats of Elizabethan ministers reveals just how informal the conduct of administration often was. The two Cecils and Walsingham used private secretaries, appointed by themselves and essentially members of their households, to transact the widest range of administrative business. This was not administration by bureaucracies, it was administration from the households of the great Tudor ministers. Such arrangements, which existed side by side with large bureaucratic machines like the Exchequer and Chancery, show that Elizabethan administrative practice combined 'household' and 'bureaucratic' elements. In view of this, and even setting aside the whole question of Elton's interpretation of medieval administration, it seems dangerous to argue that the 1530s witnessed an administrative revolution.

If Elton is wrong in seeing the 1530s as the vital period in the transition from medieval to modern methods of administration, it may also be suggested that he is looking at the whole problem in the wrong terms. The hallmark of modern administration is its use of statistics on a vast scale, as any citizen who has been plagued by official forms will readily appreciate. Medieval administration on the other hand, whatever the nature of the institutions through which it was carried out, made little or no use of statistics. The really revolutionary change which has taken place in administrative methods since the middle ages has been the application, in a systematic way, of statistics to the problems of administration. This was a change which took place very slowly, it was probably not completed until the twentieth century, but if one is looking for a particularly significant period in the transition it may be that special attention should be paid to the later seventeenth century, the Restoration era, which saw the rise of what contemporaries called 'political arithmetic' and we would call statistics. In 1701, John Arbuthnot, a distinguished mathematician and physician, forcibly stated the need for the application of statistical methods to administrative problems when he wrote:

Arithmetic is not only the great instrument of private commerce, but by it are (or ought to be) kept the public accounts of a nation; I mean those that regard the whole state of a commonwealth, as to the number, fructification of its people, increase of stock, improvement of lands and manufactures, balance of trade, public revenues, coinage, military power by sea and land, etc. Those that would judge or reason truly about the state of any nation must go that way to work, subjecting all the forementioned particulars to calculation.[1]

These remarks conjure up the modern world of rational administrative methods. Perhaps it was the age which saw the flowering of such ideas which saw the beginnings – though of course *only the beginnings* – of the real administrative revolution in English history.

It would seem, in short, that there was no revolution in government or administration in the Tudor period. Despite the important changes which took place during the century – and no one would deny that the administrative reforms of the 1530s in particular were important – the English system of government in 1600 was not *fundamentally* different from the system in 1500. Policy was still made by the Crown and administration was still carried out by a mixture of bureaucratic departments and informal agencies. The transition from medieval to modern forms of government and administration was a long, complex, and subtle process which saw control of policy pass from the hands of the Crown to those of the Crown's ministers and which saw the change from an administrative system based on primitive calculations to one founded on the sophisticated techniques of modern statistics. The first of these changes was not completed until the nineteenth century and the second until the twentieth.

The sixteenth and early seventeenth centuries, then, may not have seen 'revolutionary' changes in the nature of government and administration, but the 'strong' Elizabethan governmental system did nevertheless differ in important respects from the 'weak' rule of Edward VI and Mary and the 'unsuccessful' régimes of the first two Stuarts. It is easy to make dramatic contrasts between the governments of Elizabeth and James I. Elizabeth, who worked industriously at affairs of state and always represented the ceremonial side of monarchy to perfection, can be contrasted with the lazy James, who neglected government business in favour of hunting and presented a very undignified

[1] G. N. Clark, *Guide to English Commercial Statistics 1696–1782* (1938), xiii.

picture to the world with his shambling gait and padded clothes. The Privy Council under Elizabeth was small, efficient and composed of able men, whereas under James it grew larger and less efficient and, after Salisbury's death in 1612, contained only mediocrities and nonentities. Under Elizabeth the House of Commons was managed by a combination of judicious royal interventions and the astute control of procedure through the Speaker and the councillor-members of the House, whilst under James it was mismanaged by the King's foolish and frequent meddling in Commons' business and the government's failure to retain control of procedure. Under Elizabeth the Crown was served by a succession of great ministers, whereas James had none after 1612. In Elizabeth's reign the prerogative and common law courts worked together without friction, but James's reign saw a struggle between the common lawyers and the prerogative courts which was to continue under Charles I. Under Elizabeth government was reasonably honest and the Elizabethan patronage system worked in such a way that no one man was able to monopolize the distribution of offices and favours, whilst in James's reign there was gross corruption in the public service and the distribution of patronage came to be monopolized shamelessly by one man, the Duke of Buckingham, who enriched himself and his relatives.

This picture is largely valid if James's later years are contrasted with the high Elizabethan period – the middle part of the Queen's reign – but the situation is rather different if his rule is compared with that of Elizabeth in the 1590s. In the 1590s there were changes which show that the whole atmosphere of government was very different then from what it had been in the Queen's earlier years. Some of these changes presaged the developments of the Stuart period.

By the 1590s the Queen herself was failing. It is true that she could from time to time display bursts of her old energy and fire – as in 1597 when she trounced an insolent Polish ambassador in extempore Latin – but these were isolated episodes and as she advanced into her sixties her powers declined. The letters of her godson Sir John Harington, which provide some of the best descriptions of her in her later years, show her as an irascible and embittered old woman.[1] The ageing Elizabeth had no new ideas

---

[1] J. Harington, *Nugae Antiquae*, i (1804), pp. 235, 314–5, 318, 320–23.

to solve the pressing political, financial and social problems which were facing the country in the 1590s. Her conservatism, which had served England well for so many years was, at the end of her reign, a liability.

The decline in the Queen's personal powers can be paralleled by a decline in the government's authority in Parliament. Privy councillors were no longer able to control the Commons as effectively as before; members showed a growing truculence and turbulence; and the committee system, which had previously been exploited by councillors in the interests of the Crown now began to slip out of their control. Above all, the financial difficulties and demands of the government during these years gave the Commons a powerful weapon to use in their disputes with the Queen. All these changes can be linked with developments in the early Stuart period when the government completely 'lost the initiative' in the Commons, where, by the 1620s, procedure and committees were almost completely controlled by an opposition which showed little sympathy for the Crown's ever increasing financial problems.

By the 1590s, too, Elizabeth had lost many of her most prominent ministers and servants. Leicester died in 1588, Mildmay in 1589, Walsingham, in 1590, Hatton in 1591. Burghley, it is true, lived on, but he, like his mistress, was growing old. In the 1590s, and especially from 1592 onwards, he was constantly ill and frequently unable to leave his bed.[1] This was most unfortunate as he was still the very lynchpin of the administration. Moreover, as he aged, his growing conservatism reinforced that of his mistress. In the 1590s Elizabeth's chief minister, no less than the Queen herself, was bankrupt of new ideas in a changing world.

The last decade or so of Elizabeth's reign also saw the beginnings of that struggle between common lawyers and prerogative courts which occupied such a prominent place in the early Stuart period, and the bitter faction struggle between Essex and Robert Cecil, a contest which took heightened drama from Essex's desire to become the sole beneficiary of royal patronage. He failed, and it was left to Buckingham to achieve by the 1620s, with James's full consent, the position which Essex had craved and Elizabeth had refused in the 1590s. The Essex–Cecil struggle was accompanied

[1] C. Read, *Lord Burghley and Queen Elizabeth*, pp. 480, 485, 501, 504, 507, 514, 541–2.

by and indeed was partly the cause of the decline in political morality which was a conspicuous feature of Elizabeth's last years. That too was a foretaste of things to come. The corrupt practices which grew in Court and administration in these years became a flood during James's lax rule, reaching their apogee under Buckingham in the 1620s.

It seems clear, indeed, that the 1590s saw the beginnings of the breakdown of the high Elizabethan system of government, a breakdown which gathered force as the early Stuart period progressed until it culminated in the final rupture of relations between King and Commons in the Long Parliament and the outbreak of the Civil War in 1642.

Bibliography

THE most important works on the Queen are those of Sir John Neale, though his famous biography *Queen Elizabeth*, published as long ago as 1934 is in need of revision in the light of later research. This is especially true of the picture which it presents of the last decade of the reign, and here J. Hurstfield's *Elizabeth I and the Unity of England* (1960) and B. W. Beckingsale's brief biography, *Elizabeth I* (1963) are very useful. Several of Neale's articles contain valuable discussions of the characteristics of Elizabeth's government. Especially helpful are *The Elizabethan Age*, the Creighton Lecture in History for 1950 (published 1951), reprinted in *Essays in Elizabethan History* (1958); 'Elizabeth and the Netherlands, 1586–7', *EHR*, xlv (1930) reprinted in *Essays in Elizabethan History*; 'The via media in politics', *Essays in Elizabethan History* – originally published as 'Elizabeth I and her cold war', *Saturday Review*, 1 October 1955; and *England's Elizabeth* (Washington, D.C., 1958) reprinted in *The Age of Catherine de Medici and Essays* (1963).

There is no detailed account of the Elizabethan Privy Council, but volume i of E. P. Cheyney's *History of England* (1914) contains a good brief sketch. Many of the great ministers and courtiers who sat on the Council – Leicester and Essex, for example – await their biographers, but C. Read has produced lengthy studies of Burghley and Walsingham. His two-volume work on the former, *Mr. Secretary Cecil and Queen Elizabeth* (1955), *Lord Burghley and Queen Elizabeth* (1960), is immensely erudite, but it concentrates on the details of foreign affairs and domestic politics and is a good deal less illuminating on Burghley's attitude towards the machinery of government than J. Hurstfield's *The Queen's Wards* (1958) which contains what is in many ways the best study of Burghley and his son and successor, Robert Cecil, Earl of Salisbury. Read's other large work, *Mr. Secretary Walsingham* (3 vols., Oxford, 1925), is both comprehensive and judicious.

On Elizabeth's Parliaments there are Neale's indispensable volumes, *The Elizabethan House of Commons* (1949) and *Elizabeth I and her Parliaments* (2 vols., 1953, 1957), while Wallace Notestein, *The Winning of the Initiative by the House of Commons* (British Academy Raleigh Lecture in History, reprinted from the Proceedings of the Academy, 1924), and D. H. Willson, *The Privy Councillors in the House of Commons 1604–29* (Minneapolis, 1940), describe how the government lost control of the Lower House in the early Stuart period.

We know very little about some of the major organs of Elizabethan administration, for example about the Exchequer, but other institutions of government have been studied in detail, notably the Court of Wards, on which two major works have appeared. One of these, H. E. Bell's *Introduction to the History and Records of the Court of Wards and Liveries* (Cambridge, 1953), is a discussion of the organization of the Court, while the other, J. Hurstfield's *The Queen's Wards*, is a survey of the social consequences of feudal wardship and marriage in the Elizabethan period and also a discussion of the effects of the wardship system upon the government of the country. On the very important office of secretary of state there is F. M. G. Evans's book, *The Principal Secretary of State* (Manchester, 1923), while on the law and the law courts W. S. Holdsworth's great *History of English Law* is indispensable. Volume i (7th ed., 1956) deals with the courts, volumes iv and v (3rd ed., 1924) with the development of the law in the sixteenth and seventeenth centuries. On the Council of the North there are two pieces of work, a Historical Association pamphlet by F. W. Brooks, *The Council of the North* (1953), and the much more detailed study by R. R. Reid, *The King's Council in the North* (1921). On the Council in the Marches there is P. Williams's excellent book, *The Council in the Marches of Wales under Elizabeth I* (Cardiff, 1958). On army administration there is C. G. Cruickshank, *Elizabeth's Army* (2nd ed., Oxford, 1966), and on the navy M. Oppenheim, *A History of the Administration of the Royal Navy ... 1509 to 1660* (1896). The financial history of the reign is discussed in F. C. Dietz, *English Public Finance 1558–1641* (New York, 1932), and W. R. Scott, *The Constitution and Finance of English, Scottish and Irish Joint Stock Companies*, vol. iii (Cambridge, 1911). The figures in these books are not always reliable, but they are the only general works on the subject. G. Scott Thomson, *Lords Lieutenant in the Sixteenth Century* (1923) gives a good account of a local government office which developed during the Tudor period, while William Lambarde's *Eirenarcha*, first published in 1581 and later revised and enlarged (it had been reprinted seven times by 1610) is the classic treatise on the Elizabethan justice of the peace. On Elizabethan administration generally, both central and local, the best books are G. R. Elton, *The Tudor Constitution* (Cambridge, 1960), E. P. Cheyney, *A History of England* (2 vols., 1914, 1926), and A. L. Rowse, *The England of Elizabeth* (1950). G. R. Elton, *The Tudor Revolution in Government* (Cambridge, 1953), deals with the administrative changes of the 1530s, but his arguments have important implications for the Elizabethan period. The recent debate between Drs. G. L. Harriss and P. Williams on the one hand and Dr. Elton on the other as to the significance of the 1530s can be followed in *Past and Present* numbers 25 (July 1963), 29 (December 1964), 31 (July 1965), and 32 (December 1965).

On the structure of Elizabethan politics and the workings of the patronage system the classic work is J. E. Neale's Raleigh Lecture of 1948 to the British Academy, 'The Elizabethan Political Scene', (reprinted in *Essays in Elizabethan History*). This should be read in conjunction with W. T. MacCaffrey's article, 'Place and Patronage in Elizabethan Politics', *Elizabethan Government and Society* (eds. S. T. Bindoff, J. Hurstfield, C. H. Williams, 1961). Also important are C. Read, 'Walsingham and Burghley in Queen Elizabeth's Privy Council', *EHR*, xxviii (1913), and J. Hurstfield, 'The Succession Struggle in Late Elizabethan England', *Elizabethan Government and Society*, which deal with the faction struggles among ministers and courtiers which were so important in the politics of Elizabethan England. Material for comparing the situation under James I and Charles I with the Elizabethan political scene can be found in D. H. Willson's excellent biography *King James VI and I* (1956), in L. Stone's monumental work, *The Crisis of the Aristocracy 1558–1641* (Oxford, 1965), and in G. E. Aylmer's *The King's Servants* (1961), a study of Charles I's civil service.

The best introduction to the social and economic policies of Elizabeth's government is to be found in P. Ramsey, *Tudor Economic Problems* (1963). E. M. Leonard, *The Early History of English Poor Relief* (Cambridge, 1900), is useful on the details of legislation on the poor but inadequate on the enforcement of the law. This latter point is, however, well treated in W. K. Jordan, *Philanthropy in England 1480–1660* (1959). S. T. Bindoff discusses 'The Making of the Statute of Artificers' in *Elizabethan Government and Society*, and M. R. G. Davies deals with aspects of its enforcement in *The Enforcement of English Apprenticeship 1563–1642* (Cambridge, Massachusetts, 1956).

C. Read, ed., *Bibliography of British History, Tudor Period* (2nd ed., Oxford, 1959) provides a comprehensive list of published works.

Index

24   E11GS
      SMITH

         00